The Theory of Everything

By

Vern G. Rickey

ISBN: 0-7596-7565-1

This book is printed on acid free paper.

1stBooks - rev. 02/22/02

TABLE OF CONTENTS

SECTION—1

"THE"
"THEORY OF"
"EVERYTHING"

Two fish in the ocean look at each other and the water between them appears as space to the fish. We know that the space is filled with water, and that the fish are made of about .97% water and about .03% something else. The fish don't know this though and are not aware that they are in a medium, and are composed mostly of the medium that they are in.

The standard model of nuclear physics that is endorsed by science does not include gravity as part of nuclear theory. This has not been done on purpose and the scientific community is very much concerned about it. The reason that "Gravity" has not been included is that no particle has ever been found that can be identified as a "Graviton" as a hypothetical particle of gravity. It has been conjectured by some members of the scientific community that a "Graviton" as a particle of gravity would be a mass-less particle, similar but different in many respects to a "Photon" as a particle of light or as a "Gluon" found in the atomic nucleus. Gravity is treated as a geometrically shaped gravitational field by the "General theory of Relativity" and not as a particle. All matter radiates energy and has "Gravity", from atomic particles to the structure of Galaxies. Some scientists believe that "Gravity" as currently measured at the atomic level is so weak and feeble that the effect it would have on atomic and subatomic particles is of very little consequence anyway.

One of the things about existing theories is that each theory requires something as a mechanism for each theory that occupies what is believed to be the vacuum of empty outer space for each theory. There are basically four accepted theories and four forces as prescribed by today's science. The four forces are,

"Gravity", "The Strong Nuclear Force", "The Electro Dynamic force", and the "Electro weak force". The "Electro Dynamic" and the "Electro Weak" forces have a unifying theory. Each force has a theory or theories that more or less supports each force.

Gravity as a force, has "Newtonian mechanics" and the "General theory of Relativity". The "General theory of Relativity" treats gravity as having a stretched or warped shape to the fabric of space that dilates time and changes dimension. There is a warp or curve to the fabric of space as a space time continuum. Electro Dynamics as a force has "QED" for short or "Quantum Electro dynamics". Nuclear theory that includes the strong nuclear force has as a theory, "QCD" for short or "QUANTUM CROMODYNAMICS". The newest theories are the unification of the "Electro dynamic" and the "Electro weak" forces and could be considered as an Electro weak force theory. All of these theories work for a specific situation and all are valid theories but each theory requires a mechanism in what is believed to be the vacuum of empty outer space for each theory.

A requirement of the "General theory of Relativity" is that there be a value neither matter or field but the fabric of space that is warped into a space time continuum. Quantum electro dynamics as a theory has electro magnetic fields that occupy all of the Cosmos that carry "Photons" as particles of light. The unification of the Electro weak and Electro Dynamic forces have introduce a particle called the "Higgs particle" and the "Higgs field" as the "Higgs" mechanism. Physicists are looking for a particle called a graviton and for gravity waves as a rip or tear in the fabric of space and time. Besides the magnetic fields that carry photons as particles of light, there are strong magnetic fields for the sun, earth, jupiter and to a lesser degree all of the Planets and all matter that have nothing to do with light. Then there is the substance of the solar wind.

It becomes apparent then that what is believed to be the empty vacuum of outer space theory wise, is not so empty after all. Theoretically, the vacuum of outer space is getting pretty crowded with all the different mechanisms that supports each theory. A theory of everything would not only have to unify the four forces as a single force, but would also have to unify all the theories into one theory. It would have to go further yet and unify all the mechanisms that support each theory into a single universal mechanism.

There is another common denominator and principles of physics that will unify the forces, and bring all the theories together than the way in which the scientific community is doing in the "Big Bang" and the theory of "Grand Unification". Physicists and theorists have a theory that the four forces were equal and one force at a period of time as part of the reactionary sequence called the "Big Bang". The scientific community in visualizing a "Theory of everything", believes that there is a way to unify all existing theories into one theory but because of the nature of existing theories have not been able to put there finger on just what it is. In order to bring together a "Theory of Everything" that will unify the forces and the theories there has to be some fundamental understanding of reality.

Einstein had to give substance to space in order to account for time and dimension. He kept the speed of light constant and allowed time and dimension to change. Because of this he left space as space and yet gave it substance that he warped of curved to fit gravity as a geometric curve of space and time and it worked. In effect he implies that space has an average density that is neither matter or space but is instead a continuum of space-time which is the same through out all space. Physicist's then asserted that you did not need gravity at all because of the geometric curvature of space and time and yet they are looking for a "Graviton" as a particle of gravity.

The "Theories of Relativity" have been under attack. There are those that claim that they can disprove the theories mathematically. There are also those that are disputing the existence of a photon as a particle of light. Still these great theories stand and endure. They stand and endure because the predications made by the theories actually happen. There were experiments conducted using atomic clocks, one stationary on the ground and two in flight on a trip around the world. The clocks in flight were first carried one way with the earth's rotation, and then again in the other against the earth's rotation that confirm the dilation of time as predicted by the "Theories of Relativity". Not only was the dilation of time predicted, but also the amount of time that was dilated was predicted and confirmed by the readings of the atomic clocks. There were also further experiments carried out by the naval observatory and the U. of Maryland with one clock on the ground and one in flight to increasingly higher altitudes that also confirm the dilation of time. The dilation of time as predicted by the "Theories of Relativity" is a physical thing that has been measured and has been proven to actually happen.

There is a point that has to be made, and that is the fact that a theory was tried visualizing atomic and subatomic particles as spheres or blobs. This theory was abandoned because it could not be made compatible with the "General theory of Relativity". The "General theory of Relativity" deals with the fabric of space as a curvatures of a space time continuum. Yet experiments carried out by particle accelerators using breams of Electrons have shown the structure of the proton to be a spherical soft blob of positive charge who's dimensions have been measured.

As an illustration, if I had ten coins, I could add or subtract from the ten coins or do any number of mathematical calculations with the ten coins as long as I had coins to work with. If I were to subtract all of the coins, I would have zero or nothing physically to work with. I do not mean dividing the coins into parts, I mean subtracting all of the coins. I could use algebra as a mathematical expression and say I had a minus number of coins, but in reality I would still have physically zero coins. No matter how of what kind of mathematical calculation are done with zero, in physical reality it is still zero or nothing. The point that is being made is, if you start with physically nothing or zero, it can be added to physically, but not taken away from.

Because of this you could take the position that there are two spaces. The fabric of space which is under the tremendous explosive expansive pressure of the “Big Bang” in which Einstein showed a warp or curve in the “General Theory of Relativity” and true flat square space which in reality is zero or nothing and stretches to infinity. This true flat square space would contain no gravity, no light, no energy, no matter, has no dimension or time and yet you can place of add anything into it. Time and dimension can not be measured except as zero because there are no frames of reference to measure to or with or from. Everything in our existence, matter, energy, light, magnetic fields, gravity and the co called fabric of space like the ten coins in the illustration are contained with in this true flat square space. This is what would exist out side of the “Big Bang”. (Nothing or zero of everything to infinity) If a graviton as a particle of gravity is ever to be introduced into scientific theory as an entity, it has to be viewed in this context. There is absolutely no other way for this to be done. A graviton as a particle of gravity has to be treated like particles of matter, as a particle. It is a physical something. Quantum theories treat matter as existing as either a particle or a wave. This will be taken up further in the next section.

SECTION—2

The following is a principle of physics that is being introduced and is being termed, "DOMINANTE SPIN ROTATIONAL ORIENTATION".

If we take just the hands and the face of a clock with out the body of the clock and make them symmetrical in every way, (no numbers or distinguishing markings) it would be impossible to tell which way the clock was running except as orientated to the observer. If we view the clock from one side face on, the hands are turning clockwise. View the clock from the back of this side and the clock is turning counter clockwise. Because of this it would be impossible to tell if the clock were running clockwise or counter-clockwise except as orientated to the observer. In effect the same motion of the clock is running both clockwise and counter-clockwise at the same time. It just depends on which side of the clock you are looking at.

If we remove the hands and the face from the clock and leave just the axis of rotation as perfectly symmetrical in every way, and view this from edge on, the axis of rotation becomes a cylinder. We then make a perfectly symmetrical straight line the length of the cylinder so we can tell if the cylinder is rotating and if it is rotating to the right or to the left or not at all as orientated to an observer. We can invert the cylinder as an axis of rotation as orientated, and like the hands of the clock, the same identical spin that appeared as spinning to the right will then be spinning to the left. You can look at a perfectly symmetrical rotating cylinder and say that it is turning right from one perspective, but from another the same identical rotation will be turning left. So which direction is the cylinder turning, to the right, or to the left? Now we can physically stop the cylinder and reverse the rotation but we again have the same problem unless we remain oriented to the cylinder's rotation. If we were to close our eyes and lose orientation and then reopen them, there would be no way of saying which direction the cylinder was turning unless a rotation is designated. (There would be no way of telling if the axis of rotation had been inverted to your orientation when your eyes were closed, or it had been stopped and the rotation of the cylinder restarted in the other direction)

This is the concept of a singularity or how a duality of motion becomes a singularity of motion. If there is introduced a second cylinder then we can tell if they are spinning in the same rotational sequence or opposite of each other. If they appear to be spinning into each other, by inverting both cylinders, the same identical spin of both cylinders will then be spinning away from each other. If we invert one of the cylinders, then they will be spinning relative to each other either to the right or to the left. As long as the cylinders were perfectly symmetrical and un-distinguishabe, it would be impossible to tell which way they were rotating with out the other one as a frame of reference to orientate it to. Then all that can be told is whether they were spinning in the same or opposite rotational sequences as orientated to each other. None of the cylinders has reversed rotation at any time, which shows that any single rotational spin, is all so a dual rotational spin. If one of the cylinders is larger or smaller than the other one then they can be spin orientated relative to each other. Now if we paint a mark on one end of the cylinders white and the other end black, then we can designate which end is up say as white north and black as south. This is again a principle of Physics that is being introduced and termed "DOMINATE SPIN ROTATIONAL ORIENTATION", and will be used through out the text.

A non-rotating graviton as a tiny little "Sphere of energy" would be symmetrical in every way. There would be no way of telling anything about the little sphere of energy as far as polarity goes unless there was invoked rotation of the particle. The same rules of rotation that applied to the cylinders as an axis of rotation would apply to a graviton and the rotation of all perfectly symmetrical particles as spheres of energy.

There are two other ingredients that have to be addressed, and that is the invariance of the speed of light for all reference frames of inertia regardless of their differential relative velocities to each other, and the "Doppler" shift of the "Electro magnetic spectrum". The speed of light is constant in any direction and is the same for any and all reference frames regardless of their differential relevant velocities to each other. Yet light acts like sound in the atmosphere in that it experiences the red and blue shift of the "Electro Magnetic Spectrum" in a similar manor to sound waves. This has baffled Physicists and Scientists and although Einstein's theories of "Relativity" deal with it as a dilation of time and space, still no one knows how or why it happens. Einstein simply said that it is just a property of light but could give no reason for the consistency. The invariance of the speed of light and the "Doppler shift" of the "Electro magnetic Spectrum" will be fully taken up and explained in section Six.

Time should be mentioned here. Time is important but time is a "by product" of dimension and is a measurement of an expenditure of energy. When there is gravitational change of dimension or change of dimension by relative motion, time also changes. Time for gravitationally contracted dimensions is slow, as compared to time for expanded dimensions. For the dimensions of a sphere the three spatial dimensions should be calculated as six dimensions instead of three. The six dimensions are all from the apex of a sphere as an extension of the three spatial dimensions. These six radii of a sphere can then be increased to spherical dimensional infinity. Any two of the infinite radii of a sphere can be extended as an axis of rotation for the other four. The other four then become a three dimensional plane of rotation.

The meaning of the phrase a "Gravitational sphere of perception" will not mean much now but will be made clear later in the text. For now, as the gravitational sphere of perception contracts, dimension and time remain constant (except for accelerated motion). As the "Gravitational sphere of perception" expands, dimension and time still remain constant but is different for differential "Gravitational spheres of perception". Time and dimension for a contracted "Gravitational sphere of perception" is smaller (dimension) and slower (time) as perceived by a larger expanded "Gravitational sphere of perception".

This is fundamentally the structure for "Super Symmetry", the structure of time, and is the mechanism that will unify three of the four forces as defined by science and give an explanation as to what the fourth force is. Before this can be understood though, we have to go through the steps leading up to this like we were building a house. We have to lay foundation first, then framing, siding, and walls before we can put on the roof. Once the house is built, then we can set back and view the whole structure and it will have meaning.

A sphere is the only true fundamental geometric shape. All geometric shapes are derived from spheres. A point as a particle is a sphere that is at the limits of our perception. A sphere that is contacted to a point particle when magnified, becomes a sphere again. A point as a particle (as a sphere of energy) that is contracted to infinity, becomes a measurement of the quantitative substance as part of a Black Hole. The planets our sun and the stars are all near spheres. A raindrop is a perfect sphere and it has been determined by actual measurements that a Proton is a sphere.

Draw a circle on a piece of paper. We see the circle in two dimensions as a flat circle on the piece of paper. We draw lines as four radii on the flat circle that divides the circle into four quadrants. This is subdivided again into eight radii and again into sixteen radii. The circle is sub-divided again and again until there are x number of radii of the circle. We change the circle and view the circle as a sphere. As a sphere we can draw many more radii for the sphere than we could for the circle. We keep drawing radii for the sphere until there are so many radii that the lines all touch clear out to the circumference of the sphere, so we draw finer lines and keep drawing finer lines so we can get more radii into the sphere. The center of the sphere has long been covered as the lines overlap one another and the sphere has becomes so solid that we can not tell one line from another. So we enlarge the circumference of the sphere. The larger we get the circumference of the sphere, the more radii we can draw for the sphere. We inflate the circumference of the sphere clear out to the diameter of the earth which has a radius of about four thousand miles. We make the lines so fine that we decrease the width of the lines clear down to the dimension of a single angstrom. An angstrom as a unit of measurement is one ten billionth of a meter. We have drawn so many radii for the sphere now that we have come to a state that will have to be seen as being random and chaotic. If we divide all the infinite radii that are four thousand miles long into strings of single spheres that have a diameter of one angstrom per. sphere, then all the un-calculable spheres that are one angstrom in diameter are in a state of random chaos. If we go further still and increase the infinite radii of the spheres to the radius of our sun, which is about four hundred and fifty thousand miles long, then random chaos is random chaos compounded to infinity. (Our sun is just one very small star of billions in our "Milky Way Galaxy" and there are many more billions of galaxies) The point that is being made is, a single sphere that is one angstrom in diameter relative to a sphere that has a diameter of about eight thousand miles, is in a state of random chaos. This illustration using the earth as a model shows the difference between geometry as a geometric shape of something and particles in random chaos as the shape of something.

The "General theory of Relativity" describes the shape of the fabric of space as a geometric line of curvature that changes physical dimension and dilates time. The illustration of the infinite radii demonstrates that geometry only holds for large dimensions and if you try to take geometry as a shape of things to extremely small dimension such as an angstrom, you will run in to a state of "Random chaos". You could determine the shape of a single grain of sand, but this would not give you the shape of a shovel full, a truckload, or all the sand on all the beaches of the whole earth. The "Theories of Relativity" deal with Mass, Energy and the curvature of time and dimension on a large scale as the geometric shape of things. “Quantum nuclear theories” on the other hand deal with mass and energy at extremely small dimensions (Not gravity) that are in a random chaotic state. Quantum nuclear theories work because they are calculated on the law of averages or the law of probabilities. This law simply states that if you do something over and over again enough times, what you are trying to do will happen soon or later. There will be a pattern that will emerge.

As an example, if I flip a penny ten times, I will have a random chaotic pattern of heads and tails in that every time I flip the penny ten times, the pattern of heads and tails will be different. If I make a record and keep track as I flip the penny and flip the penny enough times, say about a thousand times, the number of heads and tails will be almost equal at about five hundred apiece. This is basically how the “law of averages” or the “law or probabilities” works.

The “Theories of Relativity” are proven theories that work and as much of the theories that can be tested, have proven to be accurate. Quantum nuclear theories also work and are proven theories but do not include gravity as part of Quantum nuclear theories. The only way to include gravity as a quantum nuclear theory is to view the shape of a gravitational field as being composed of particles of gravity. This is a “Graviton” as a tiny little particle or sphere of energy. A Graviton as a particle of gravity of a gravitational field would have to contract, and if a graviton as a particle of gravity can contract, it will also under the right circumstances expand.

Place two non-rotating spheres together of equal radii as the fabric of space and a single radius of both spheres will form a perfect straight line no matter what position the two spheres are in. (Do not be concerned about time just yet) Place three non-rotating spheres together and they form a perfect equilateral triangle. Place four together and they form a pyramid. Place four together on a flat surface and they form a square. Place four more on top of those and they form a cube. Put two spheres together and you can place four more around them making a five-sided figure or star shape. Put one sphere on a flat surface and you can place six more around the one sphere. Place twelve more around those for a total of nineteen and it forms a sextant or six-sided figure all from equal spheres. (Chinese checkers) You can add row after row around the six-sided figure and it always takes only six more spheres per row and the figure is always six-sided. This could be extended as a slice of the fabric of space clear across the cosmos and it would still only be a six-sided figure. The spheres as tiny little particles of energy of the "Gravitational Aether" are at all times in solid contact with each other and each sphere is under the tremendous explosive expansive pressure of a "Bang or the Big Bang" to expand but are contained by the presence of the medium to a certain pressure as a force of compression. This could be viewed as an invisible cosmic foam that fills the whole cosmos that is under pressure to expand.

Place two non-rotating spheres together of different radii and a single radius of each sphere will still form a perfect straight line. Place three spheres together all of different radii and any shaped triangle of infinite dimensions can be made using the radii of the spheres. It follows then that using up to an infinite number of spheres, and up to an infinite number of radii and lengths of radii of the spheres, that any warp, curve, distortion, or multiple dimensions of time and space can be derived at.

Now go back to the nineteen spheres as a six-sided figure (Chinese checkers again) and stack spheres on top of them into columns. If the columns are twisted either to the right or to the left, the six-sided figure becomes a circular cylinder. This is really nothing new, rope as a column of spheres is twisted either to the right, or to the left as the lay of the rope. What is new is the conception that the fabric of space has a chirality or helical twist either to the right, or to the left, as the texture or grain of the fabric of space itself.

To see how a Graviton could be visualized as a particle of Gravity, we have to place Gravitons in true flat square space as the shape of an imaginary gravitational field and under the explosive expansive pressure of the "Big Bang". Physicists use a model to illustrate the imaginary shape of a gravitational field by stretching a piece of rubber sheet over a large frame and inserting a lead or iron ball into the center of the stretched piece of rubber. By greasing the surface of the rubber to near zero friction, a marble on the surface of the rubber sheet will illustrate how a satellite supposedly stays in an elliptical orbit around a celestial sphere. If we dim the lights down low and view the model from over head, the stretched rubber sheet appears flat with the marble spinning around the iron or lead ball in a tipped elliptical orbit that also looks flat. This in a manor of speaking shows how the fabric of space is stretched into the shape of a gravitational field as put forth by the "General theory of Relativity". The difference is that the stretched rubber sheet and the marble in its tipped elliptical orbit in the real physical world are actually flat and square to a great circle of the apex of the iron or lead ball and not curved or tipped.

In order to bring this into three dimensions and visualize a Graviton as a particle of Gravity of a "Gravitational field", if we draw a line from the edge of the stretched curved rubber to the iron or lead ball, it will naturally be a curved line. This as an illustration more of less shows the curve of space as described by the "General theory of Relativity" although the lines have to be different in the real physical world. The rubber sheet is thicker at the outer most edges of the sheet and thinner where it is stretched around the ball at the center, so we will draw the line on top of the rubber and in three dimension. The line will be cylindrical and uniform in diameter the entire length of the line, following the curve from the edge of the rubber sheet to and following the curve of the ball at its apex. Next we divide the line into a string of spheres that have the same diameters as the diameter of the cylindrical line.

Now the only way to get the curved line to run to the apex of the iron or lead ball as a gravitational vector and flatten the rubber sheet is to change the diameters of some of the string of spheres. By contracting the diameters of spheres closer to the ball, we can get more spheres into the cylindrical line, which will then shorten the line and curve it back up and to the apex of the iron or lead ball. This changes the shape of the line into a curved tapered cylindrical shape that still has curvature. Although as a string of curved points, they are now all pointing to and on a flat plane with a great circle formed by a radius from the apex of the Iron or lead ball. We have also physically flattened the stretched rubber sheet and leveled the tipped elliptical orbit of the marble on to a flat plane that is also on a plane with a great circle formed by a radius of the iron or lead ball. This then would be the true physical shape of a gravitational vector in reality. The true gravitational vector is a curved line that is on a flat plane with a great circle formed by a radius from the apex of the iron or lead ball. The line as put forth by the "General theory of Relativity" deals with this as a curved line that stretches the dimension of the fabric of space but in physically reality the line is straight. If we view the line as being composed of random chaotic particles, and still retain some symmetry as to particle diameters and their placement in the field, then the line as a gravitational vector does not have to be curved which in the true physical world it is not.

We start out at the edge of the rubber sheet at the larger spheres and use the diameter of each successive sphere as an equal unit of measurement. By doing so, it becomes apparent that spheres closer in to the ball are at a different, physical dimension, energy level, and dimension of time than spheres farther out from the ball. By calculating each different diameter of the spheres both large and small as being an equal unit of the same dimension, then spheres that are closer in are at a different true flat square dimension than the actual dimension of the spheres. The same is true if the diameter of each sphere is calculated as an equal increment of time. It would take longer to transit the dimension of the contracted spheres than it would the same true flat square space dimension. As an example of this, if we have ten spheres one inch in diameter, the length would be ten inches. If we have ten spheres 1/4 inch in diameter, the length would be two and one half inches. By treating all spheres as equal units of time and dimension, it would take four times as long to transit the 1/4-inch diameter spheres as it would the one-inch spheres. The Gravitational field is made up of "Gravitons" of different sizes that are packed solid as little spheres of energy. The smallest spheres are closer to the iron or lead ball and then are progressively tapered out to larger spheres at the perimeters of the field to the inverse square rule.

So far this illustration has no motion. Nothing works or is moving, everything, all the spheres are like a big sack of tiny little different sized marbles just setting there. It does show though how Gravitons as spheres of energy as the fabric of space when progressively contracted can show the physical shape of curvature of a "Gravitational field" that has no motion and is frozen in time. All spheres of energy as Gravitons as the fabric of space would not follow straight lines to a celestial sphere, but rather are arranged in a random chaotic pattern. Spheres of the same dimensions do not fit together uniformly anyway let along spheres of smaller dimensions and Pi is infinite. Pi has been taken to over 100 million decimal places and beyond by computers and it always ends up with a non-divisible number. Pi by itself then is infinite and Pi to the square of the distance or the inverse square is infinity compounded. To achieve motion and start time then a Graviton as a sphere of energy as a particle of Gravity, would have to move into a contractual caving in flow following a random chaotic pattern, but as a dimensional measurement to the inverse square the same as light.

This at first looks completely impossible but there is a "principle of physics" that will be introduce that shows how this can happen. We also have to show the mechanism that contracts Gravitons as spheres of energy into a contractual flow that forms a Gravitational field, show where they go and how matter can physically move through the medium and still not violate the basic principles of "The theories of Relativity". In order for a Graviton as a particle of Gravity of a Gravitational field to fully function, it would also have to contract to a singular point of infinite contraction as a single dimensional entity of one motion, as the quantitative substance of a "Black Hole". To date the scientific community has not identified a particle from their particle zoo that they will call a "Graviton" or phenomena that can be called "Gravity waves".

Einstein also developed the principle of the photoelectric cell in which he viewed light as a particle. A "Photon". A "Photon" or particle of light was seen as a tiny high-speed billiard ball flying around at 186,270 miles per. second knocking electrons out of metal plates. Because of this a "Photon" was seen as having no inertia, zero mass and as a particle that is viewed today as the force carrier in "Quantum theories".

On the other hand Mr. James Clerk Maxwell had already introduced the "Electro-magnetic spectrum" that saw the propagation of light as waves of varying frequencies and intensities carried by an "Electro-magnetic field". The Electro-magnetic field traveled at the same speed as the wavelengths of light, which again is 186,270 miles a second. All of space is to be permeated with "Electro-magnetic fields" that carry Photons as particles of light in waves. Physicists today view light as a dual entity, existing in one context as a particle, and in the other as a wave of the "Electro Magnetic Spectrum". This same duality as a particle and a wave has been carried over into Quantum theories.

Quantum Electro dynamics (QED) has been tested to twelve decimal points or better and is believed by many physicists to be a role model for all of the other theories in science. Quantum theories work beautifully. Quantum theories have had great success in almost every field of endeavor. Quantum theories are basically measuring devices that work on the law of probabilities or the law of averages. Quantum theories view particles in the same context as light as a dual entity either as a particle or as a wave. The particle in some cases acts like a wave and in other instances it acts like a particle. This is partly what the trouble is. A motor boat on a lake is both a wave and a particle. Yet in Quantum theories the motor boat as a particle disappears and becomes only the wave or the wave partially disappears and becomes what seems to be only the motor boat with little or no wave. The transformation from particle to wave and from wave to particle is a true physical thing that happens. This right to day is as baffling to physicists as the invariance of the speed of light and the Doppler shift of the Electro magnetic spectrum. If you view just the wave as the particle you have the motion of the boat as a wave but you do not really have the position of the boat as a particle. The wave is a wave of one thing and the particle is a particle of something else and yet they intertwine, one becoming the one and the one becoming the other. Waves, any kind of waves even standing waves are waves of something. There has to be a physical something that is the structure and substance of the wave, and there has to be a physical something as an energy source that is responsible for and makes the wave. You can not say it is just a quantum wave and write it off as that. A quantum wave or wavelet as they are called is hypothetically a wave of nothing. If you view waves as hypothetical waves of nothing then you are at a dead end and can go no further with your theories. Because of this, much of science today in searching for a "Theory of everything" is at a dead end.

Back in the nineteenth century it was believed that there was a "Luminiferous Aether" that was responsible for the propagation of light. Physicists were not able to perform any test that would show divinations of the speed of light relative to the motion of the earth that would support the existence of the "Luminiferous Aether". A Mr. Albert Michelson invented an instrument called an Optical Interferometer. He and a Mr. Edward Morley another prominent Physicist of the period, preformed the tests that to the scientific community's satisfaction disproved the "luminiferous Aether theory".

We start this out and view "Photons" in exactly the same context as we did "Gravitons" with all the particles packed solid like a big sack of tiny little marbles as the "Gravitational Aether". They fill the whole cosmos, non-rotating, uni-directional and each particle is under the tremendous explosive expansive pressure of the "Big Bang" to expand but are contained by the presence of the medium to a uniform pressure. When a particle or a band of particles expands, it can be detected as a single "Photon" or waves of "Photons" as waves of the "Electro magnetic Spectrum". When a "Photon" is neutral or contracting, it appears only as the color black and can not be detected as a single particle. The black neutral and contracting cycle of "Photons" covers all frequencies of the "Electro magnetic spectrum" and is the black body effect known in physics that absorbs all radiation. In explaining the wave function of "Photons" we will use any wave of monochromatic light first, but any frequency or frequencies of the "Electro magnetic spectrum" would be propagated in a similar manor. The propagation of a typical wavelength of monochromatic light has all the particles packed solid as the fabric of space with each particle under the explosive expansive pressure of the "Big Bang" and again this is seen in exactly the same way that "Gravitons" were shown.

A spherical band of particles of the medium expands as a shell around an energy source as the first expanding band, and are detected as "Photons" of the "Electro magnetic Spectrum" by there expansion. A second spherical band of particles as a shell outside of and larger than the first expanding band, does not expand or contract, but remains black and neutral and moves away from the first expanding band as the moving band in-concert to the first expanding band. A third band of particles as a shell outside the second moving band, contracts in response to the motion of the moving band and also remains black as it contracts. The first expanding band then contracts and becomes black, this allows the second moving band which is still neutral and black, to move back in-concert to the first band. This allows the third contracted band as a black shell to expand and is detected as waves of Photons of the "Electro magnetic spectrum" by their expansion. The greater circumference of each successive shell of particles to the inverse square dilutes the energy of each successive wave and the waves lose intensity.

The thickness of each expanding shell as a band determines the frequency of the "Electro Magnetic Spectrum". Very thin shell's as bands are high frequency Gamma, X and cosmic rays. Thicker shells such as visible light, the infrared clear out to the long length of radio waves are progressively lower frequencies.

A single "Photon" transmits its energy over a distance similar to the energy of a string of bowling balls. Hit the end of a string of bowling balls with a ball and the ball on the other end will jump or move. The expansion of a single "Photon" is detected as a "Photon" and the expansion of this single particle induces a physical motion of a string of "Photons" as particles of the "Gravitational Aether" that remain black and neutral. The movement of the neutral string of black "Photons" induces contraction of another second single black "Photon" that remains black and contracts. The first "Photon" then contracts, becomes black and the string of black neutral "Photons" then move back toward the first "Photon". This allows the second single contracted "Photon" that is black to expand and is detected as a "Photon" of the "Electro magnetic Spectrum" by its expansion.

The cycle then repeats its self. The expansion and contraction is at the speed of light and like the frames of a motion picture, the repeated cycles of expansion and contraction give the impression that the same photon is jumping back and forth and is a moving particle. It is the contracting expanding energy of a photon that moves from photon to photon or a string of black neutral moving photons at the speed of light and not the actual particles themselves. This gives the illusion of a "Photon" as a particle that jumps from one place to another instantly at the speed of light with no acceleration or de-acceleration when they do not. In quantum theories "Photons" are viewed as being absorbed by some particles and emitted by other particles in different cases. Here again it is not the particle that is being absorbed or emitted, but the energy of the particles contraction or expansion and then the particle goes black and can not be detected. This system of "Photon motion" does not change anything at all in Quantum theories. Quantum theories can and will still view "Photons" as particles jumping from place to place and "Photons" as being emitted or absorbed by other particles. This is also why a "Photon" as a particle has acted like it has no mass and is why Physicists have viewed a "Photon" as a mass less particle.

Light is polarized in that there are waves and troughs to the propagation of light. This has been taken as proof that a "Photon" has spin, yet experiments preformed at Oxford and Seattle in confirming a prediction of the "Electro weak theory", could find no rotation to the left of light as predicted by the theory as it passed threw bismuth vapor. This at first put the "Electro weak theory "into serious jeopardy. A new experiment in 1978 was performed at Stanford. This experiment verified the predications of the electro weak theory but in an entirely different way. In this experiment, "Electrons" were used instead of "Photons". It will be found that Oxford and Seattle were right about not finding spin to "Photons". The reason they could find no spin is that a "Photon" does not have spin but electrons and positrons that confirmed the electro weak theory do.

SECTION—3

Now we can take the big sack of tiny different sized little marbles that were viewed as "Gravitons", and the big sack of tiny little expanding contracting marbles that were viewed as "Photons", and put them all together. This will make one big sack of tiny little expanding and contracting marbles as the "Gravitational Aether" that fills all the Cosmos. This allows the conception of a "Photon" as a particle that contracts and expands to be similar to that of a "Graviton" that has to contract. Contraction of any sphere is to the inverse square, and expansion of a sphere is to the square of the distance. All frequencies of the "Electro magnetic Spectrum" as light are propagated to the inverse square. A "Gravitational field" and the contraction of a "Gravitational field" are also to the inverse square or to the square of the distance. The propagation of "Light" and the contraction of a "Gravitational field" both to the inverse square is a symmetrical pattern or a link between light as a "Photon" and gravity as a "Graviton".

The presentation of a "Gravitational field" is still inert, frozen in time and has no motion. There has to be two motions for a "Graviton" as a particle of a "Gravitational field" to function that are not understood. The first is apparent as the motion of mass or matter, say as the earth in its orbit around the sun. The second and the motion that is not understood, is the motion of "Gravitons" as the quantitative substance of a "Gravitational Field". In order to achieve both motions, a second principle of physics has to be introduced. This second principle of physics is a form of "Super Symmetry" that will also unify three of the four forces as one, and explain what the forth force is.

This is a common denominator and or what has been termed "Super-Symmetry", and is a second principle of Physics that is being introduced and termed "GRAVITATIONAL AETHER INTERPHASE". This principle of Physics has to be introduced partly because existing theories have so many different phenomena in what has been believed to be the so called vacuum of empty outer space that there just isn't room for all of them unless some provisions are provided. (It isn't feasible to have Gravitons, Photons, the Higgs particle, the substance that constitute magnetic fields, the fabric of space, the solar wind, etc. all occupying the same space and not have a symmetrical system for them all to fit and work together). There has to be some kind of order for all these fields of particles. Along with this, there has to be a mechanism that allows Gravitons as particles of a Gravitational field to contract in onto each other to the point that they form a contractual flow to the inverse square into a celestial sphere and then back out again as something else forming the shape of a gravitational field. They would also have to contract in certain circumstances as a singularity of motion that will become and is the quantitative substance that is a "Black Hole". It follows that if a "Gravitational field" is composed of particles, (Gravitons) then other fields would also have to be viewed as fields of particles. A "Magnetic field" would have to be composed of "Magnetic particles" and the "Gluon fields" found in the nucleus of the elements would also have to be seen as being composed of "Gluon field particles". In fact any field of any type would have to be seen as being composed of some type of particle. The fields have to be something, and everything that has ever been broken down to it's simplest component has ended up as being composed of some type of particles. Fields to not change like some particles do as first a wave and then as particles or as particles and then as Waves. A magnetic field is a magnetic field and obeys certain laws for the field. The magnetic field in some instances can be turned on and off where as a gravitational field is permanent for it's mass.

To gain and understanding of the principle of physics being introduced and termed "Gravitational Aether interphase", we have to expand particles as tiny little spheres of energy as "Gravitons" up from the sub-atomic level. We can then visualize them as objects that we can see and relate to at our level of perception. Things at the atomic and subatomic level are so infinitesimally tiny and small, that it is not feasible to try and visualize actual dimension there. Physicists use logarithmic numbers for this purpose and have measured and weighed most if not all atomic and subatomic particles but still it is not the same as visualizing objects. Also some things at the atomic or sub-atomic level are in a random chaotic state as was shown by the structure of a sphere. Pi is infinite and Pi to the square of the distance or the inverse square is infinity compounded. Because of this then do not lose perception of just how fantastically small the entities we will be talking about really are by the imaginary blown up illustration that will be presented. The illustration presented is strictly for reference at our level of perception that gives us a sense of changing physical dimension, that which without would be extremely difficult.

Let's say then that as a blown up imaginary illustration that we can relate to, we draw several spheres as circles on a piece of paper. We draw four spheres that the radii of the spheres deploy them as a square and three more as a triangle. There will be true flat square space between the spheres. The true flat square space between the spheres will vary depending on the arrangement and position of the spheres. If we were to give spin to and contract another circle enough as a sphere of energy, it would fit into or interphase (not a misprint and not interface, but interphase) between the larger spheres. Spin under a force of compression contracts energy. A non-spinning release of energy such as the detonation of an explosive or the light from a lamp as an energy source is propagated outward in expanding spheres from the energy source to the square of the distance as measured one way, and to the inverse square the other. A spinning source of energy such as a hurricane, a tornado or a whirlpool in water under a force of compression, contracts energy as angular momentum into a vortex with the greatest energy along an axis of rotation. This is basically the principal of physics that is being introduced and is termed "Gravitational Aether interphase".

Non rotating particles of "Gravity" (Gravitons, photons, or gravaphotons) that are under the explosive expansive pressure of the "Big Bang", are under this explosive expansive force as a force of compression. A particle that is given spin and is under a force of compression, will contract as a vortex along an axis of rotation as angular momentum until it has contracted to a dimension that it will fit into or interphase into the true flat square space between larger particles of Gravity. Particles of gravity then are said to be in a state or have reached a stage of "Gravitational Aether interphase". Gravitational particles that have been contracted and have spin are under great tension to expand if they lose their spin. The particles all have a constant value that changes with a ratio of physical dimension to energy. More expanded particles have less potential energy but occupy a greater volume of true flat square space. More contracted particles have much greater potential energy but occupy a smaller volume of true flat square space. Spheres of energy as gravitational particles of the fabric of space in true flat square space would then under certain circumstances contract to the point of a single directional dimensional motion, that is the quantitative substance that forms a "Black Hole". The actual ratio of the physical contraction as dimension to energy may be much greater than has been shown in the illustration of the spheres, but it does show how the basic structure of the principle as a principle of physics termed "Gravitational Aether Interphase" is structured.

SECTION—4

The string and super-string nuclear theories see matter as tiny one dimensional resonating vibrating strings, in multi-dimensional space that are strung together forming loops and strings that make up the atomic nucleus of matter. These string and super-string nuclear theories all incorporate multi-dimensional space that utilize from ten to twenty six dimensions with the dimensions under a theoretical phenomena known as compactification. Compactification allows all the extra dimensions to be curled up out of sight from us except the three spatial dimensions and one of time of our existence. It has been found sense there formulation that there are literally thousands of similar multi-dimensional combinations of these string theories that can be used but most are plagued by infinities. The multi-dimensions used in string theory are all abstract hypothetical mathematical dimensions that have never been observed in nature. They are an exercise in higher mathematics. Where as the dilation of time and dimension as put forth by the "Theories of Relativity" are an observed and documented phenomena that have been proven to actually happen.

A "Photon" is theoretically seen in current "Quantum theories" as being mass-less and knocking electrons out of metal plates in the photoelectric effect. Small thick zinc plates are attached to the hulls of steel ships that are in salt water and are placed there to guard against an electrical effect called electrolysis. Electrolysis in steel ships are small electric currents that are in the steel of steel ships that flow from the ship into salt water which is a very good conductor of electricity. These small electric currents can cause great damage to that part of the steel shell plate of the ship that is immersed in salt water in that the metal is carried away by the passage of these small electric currents and will eventually destroy the plating of the ship. Zinc is a much better conductor of electricity than iron or steel so when small zinc plates are attached to the hull of the ship, the small electric currents flow from the zinc into the salt water and not from the steel of the ship. The zinc plates are eventually destroyed but this prevents great damage in the form of pitting and deterioration of the metal hull of the ship from electrolysis. In the electrolysis effect, electrons are flowing as small electric currents from the zinc plates into the salt water that also carry whole zinc atom along as well. The small thick zinc plates are completely destroyed over a period of time but the steel plates of the ship that are immersed in saltwater are essentially undamaged. A small part but not all of the electric currents found in metal vessels is due to the photoelectric effect of sunlight falling on the exposed metal of the vessel.

On the other hand sunlight falling on a solar panel or light focused onto the chip in a CCD camera does no harm to the metal of either the solar panel or the chip in the CCD camera. Solar panels can be used for years producing electric currents as a power source that flow in and from the panel with little or no apparent damage to the panel. This refutes the hypothesis that electrons are knocked out of metal plates by photons when electrons are formed in solar panels or in the conversion of photons to electrons in the function of a CCD camera. If they were, there would be deterioration of the metal as in the electrolysis effect when there is not. Because of this, the following is given as an explanation as to how the energy of a "Photon" becomes an Electron.

The energy of an expanding "Photon" (gravaphoton) as a particle of the fabric of space that has been presented earlier by the author expands on the surface of a solid state substance. The expansion as the expanding cycle of a wavelength of the electromagnetic spectrum is changed by contact with the magnetic field on the surface of the solid state substance. Particles of the wave (Photons as particles of the gravitational aether) do not always cycle in the cycle of expansion and contraction as waves of the "Electro magnetic spectrum" when they interact with the surface of a solid state substance. This is extremely important to understand. Instead a "Photon" (gravaphoton) as a non-rotating spherical particle of the fabric of space with in the magnetic field on the surface of the solid state substance, dents or deforms into a long ellipse and starts to spin. The long spinning ellipse then rebounds back to a sphere, to an oblate spheroid, back to a sphere and then to a long ellipse again in a spinning cycle. The particle is powered and goes through the cycle in a synchronized sympathetic resonance to the explosive expansive pressure of compression of the "Big Bang" expansion of the fabric of space. In changing from a sphere to a long spinning ellipse, then back to a sphere and then to an oblate spheroid, the particle spinning in the cycle, does not change quantitative dimensional value (expand or contract) but as a sphere of energy it does change physical shape. This change in physical shape changes physical dimensions (the three spatial dimensions change with the cycle of the particle) and time varies with the change of dimension.

The distorting spinning "Gravitational particle" has become an electron or a string particle of matter or a "Super-string", only the particle is not a string, but a cycling distorting sphere of spinning energy. When the particle is a long ellipse that has spin, it has contracted rotational leverage over gravitons as expanded non-rotating particles of the fabric of space. Gravitational particles of the fabric of space under the expansive "Big Bang" pressure are pushed into the spinning ellipse by the pressure and forced to spin in the same rotational sequence by the greater rotational leverage of the cycling particle as a long spinning ellipse. When gravitational particles are forced to spin in the same rotational sequence they will interfere with each other and contract. Gravitational particles (gravitons, gravaphotons) that have reached a certain state or stage of contraction with spin, become "Magnetic particles" that will then interphase or fit into the true flat square space between the spherical expanded gravitons that make up the fabric of what we call space.

In the spinning cycle as a long skinny ellipse, a sphere, and then an oblate spheroid, the deforming photon (gravaphoton, string, super-string), what ever you want to call it at the nucleus of the reaction, functions as a tiny little pump. The little pump is powered and responding in a synchronized sympathetic resonance to the explosive expansive pressure of the "Big Bang" as a force of compression. The little pump is spinning into and forms a gravitational vortex of contracting gravitons as particles in the fabric of space. "Gravitons" (Photons, gravaphotons) as particles of the fabric of space when forced to spin all in the same direction will contract and form a vortex as a gravitational field. When contracted, gravitational particles interphase in between expanded gravitational particles and become "Magnetic particles". "Magnetic particles" are then said to be in a state of "Gravitational Aether interphase". "Magnetic particles" will then be ejected from either the north or South Pole of the super-string.

As the ejected "Magnetic particles" with there greater leverage and spin pass through and in between "Gravitons" as particles of the fabric of space, they give NON-rotating "Gravitational particles" a fractional or partial twist all in the same rotational sequence. The fractional spin or twist all in the same rotational sequence induces fractional or a partial contraction of the "Gravitational particles". The direction of flow of the ejected "Magnetic particles" from the super-string as one flowing north and the other flowing south, determines the polarity of strings or super-strings of the same rotational sequence as either an Electron or a Positron. "Magnetic particles" ejected from the pole into the true flat square space between gravitational particles of the medium, are carried back in a curve toward the strings other pole. The trajectory of magnetic particles through gravitational particles is curved or bent back toward the string or super-strings other pole by the partial contraction of gravitational particles induced by the fractional spin or twist given to them by the passage between them of magnetic particles. This fractional twist or partial spin results in a caving in contracting motion of gravitons as particles of the "Gravitational Aether" under the "Big Bang" expansive pressure pushing or moving them toward the nucleus as the gravitational field of an Electron or a positron. This results in a dual unified cycle of "Magnetic particles" and the contracting motion of gravitational particles forming the gravitational and magnetic fields of an electron or a positron.

"Magnetic particles" with their greater contracted rotational leverage over gravitational particles are the mechanism that contracts gravitons as particles of the "Gravitational Aether" into the shape of a "Gravitational field" for electrons and positrons. (This is for dipole magnetic atomic particles only at the micro level and not gravitational fields at the macro level). Gravitational particles as they are contracted by the passage of magnetic particles again are pushed toward the super string by the explosive expansive pressure of the "Big Bang". This mechanism allows an Electron or a positron to physically move through the medium by contracting "Gravitons" (gravaphotons) as the fabric of space of the solid state substance, and what we view as empty outer space. The particle has become a free electron or positron. The photon, (graviton, gravaphoton, string, super-string, whatever) as a sphere of energy in the cycle as a spinning ellipse, sphere, oblate spheroid is physically changing spatial dimensions on an infinite scale. This then could be construed so as to validate the rational of some parts of the string and super-string nuclear theories that incorporate multi-dimensions in their theories. Multi-dimensions really do exist but instead of a specific number of dimensions, the dimensions possible are infinite.

The energy of a "Photon", when in a particle state as an "Electron" or a "Positron", can physically move through the "Gravitational Aether" as a medium. The energy of an "Electron", when in the energy state as a "Photon", can not physically move through the medium. The energy of an electron when in the wave state as a "Photon", moves through the gravitational medium as waves of the "Electro Magnetic Spectrum". The energy of the cycling deforming "Photon" (Gravaphoton call it a string or super-string) at the nucleus of the particle as either and Electron or a Positron, can revert back to and function as "Photons" as contracting expanding waves of the "Electro Magnetic spectrum". The energy of an Electron can also revert back to the expanding contracting "Photon" energy as waves of the "Electro Magnetic spectrum" and then reform some where else again as an "Electron". In fact any of the weird or bizarre antics of an "Electron" or a "Photon" can be explained by this system. (Such as an "Electron" as a particle splitting into two waves of the "Electro Magnetic Spectrum", passing through two extremely small holes or slits at the same time as waves, refracting around and reforming as an electron again etc.) An electron or positron accelerated by a force to a higher relative motion is at a higher rotational energy state, and will leave a trail of expanding "Magnetic particles" as energy that are detected in the bubble chamber of a particle accelerator. An electron also has what has been termed spin up and spin down. This is just a matter of flipping the electron over and it will spin the other way. This again is part of the principle of physics introduced and termed "DOMINANTE SPIN ROTATIONAL ORIENTATION".

Leptons are single spin particles in that the "Magnetic and Gravitational particles" of the fields all spin in the same orientated rotational sequence. Magnetic particles as a field being more contracted than gravitational particles all spin opposite of and induce a fractional or partial rotation as contraction of gravitational particles of the field. They are said to have chirality or handedness. The whole electron as a complete particle (particle and wave of the Gravitational Aether) is constantly moving internally. "Magnetic particles" as well as "Gravitational particles" of space, are all like a bunch of well ordered different sized infinitesimally tiny small ball bearings that fit together, expand, contract, and distort in a cycle, in sympathetic synchronization to the expansive "Big Bang" pressure of the "Gravitational Aether". Each particle with in the system has partial spin as contraction or full spin as interphase and is moving in its proper motion, place, and time. It could be said in a manor of speaking that the cycling sphere of energy (photon, super-string, etc) as an electron or positron is bouncing in and out of shape like a tiny little primordial rubber ball that is spinning and distorting in rhythmic syncopation to the explosive expansive pressure of the “Big Bang”. The ball will react to waves of the electromagnetic spectrum either by expanding and contracting as a “Photon”, or distorting into the ellipse, sphere, and oblate spheroid cycle as an electron or positron that can then physically move through the medium.

As evidence that “Magnetic particles” as matter orientated all spin in the same rotational sequence, when a charged particle, moves through a “Magnetic field” at right angles to the magnetic field, there is an unexplained force that is at right angles to both the particle and the “Magnetic field”. This force within a “Magnetic field” steers the particle into a curved path within the field. The charged particle will then be curved into a circular path and stay within the field. The particle can then be accelerated to great velocities with in the field. This principle, that a magnetic field will turn or curve the trajectory of a charged particle, was first used by E. O. Lawrence in the development of the cyclotron. This force is the singular rotational spin of “Magnetic particles” orientated as a matter magnetic field. An Electron as a singularity of motion has internal torque in one direction only and continually spins even when it is flipped over. When two or more Electrons come together and try to mesh, their “Magnetic particles” spinning in the same rotational sequence strongly repel each other. This repulsion to fly apart is electron pressure and in an anti-matter existence with the spin of a positron as dominate, would be positron pressure. This then is part of the first stage of “Gravitational Aether interphase” as the contraction of a gravitational particle and partially unifies Gravity as a force and “Quantum Electro Dynamics”. (A Photon and a Graviton are the same particle).

The second stage of contraction is to the “Electro weak force” as part of the same common denominator of multi-dimensional gravitational contraction. There are three types of

Leptons and three types of Neutrinos and their anti-particles. These are an Electron, a Muon and a Tau and their anti-particles. There are then the Neutrinos as an Electron Neutrino, a Muon Neutrino, a Tau Neutrino, and their anti-particles. It is believed that a true Muon mirror image does not exist because of what is known as parity or mirror violation by the "Electro weak force".

SECTION—5

The "General theory of Relativity" describes the curvature of space and dilation of time, as an explanation of the fabric of space warping or distorting forming the geometric shape of a gravitational field in continuum. The scientific community has been satisfied with this presentation, in that it is believed that the shape of a gravitational field is enough for gravity to function. If we introduce "Gravitons" as particles of space or gravity and contracted gravitons as the shape of a gravitational field, then it becomes apparent that it is not enough for there to be just the shape of a gravitational field for gravity to function. In order for a gravitational field as a field of gravitons to function and experience time, there has to be a movement or motion to particles of the fabric of space. The fabric of space as particles has to physically move. There has to be "Graviton motion" as a contraction of "Gravitational particles" into matter as presented earlier by the structure of an electron or positron.

The "Special theory of Relativity" deals with matter accelerated to a constant velocity. Rods are shortened in the line of travel and material accelerated to a constant velocity in a particle accelerator is flattened and takes the form of a pancake. Time dilates or slows and Physicist have to take into account the relativistic effects of particles at extreme velocities in there calculations. The "Special theory of Relativity" deals with matter at a constant velocity only but it has to be acceleration to the constant velocity that produces the relativistic effects. The "General theory of Relativity" goes further and deals with the acceleration of matter as acceleration that the special theory does not. This includes the effects of a gravitational field. Acceleration and the force of a gravitational field are seen as exactly one and the same thing, there being no difference between the two. Acceleration is measured as G-s of force based on the strength of the earth's gravity, say one, two, three or more G-s of force.

Motion of matter then is singular in that motion appears to effect only a single dimension and time for that dimension and that is in the line of travel. Again, rods shorten and matter accelerated by a particle accelerator to a constant velocity takes the form of a pancake. A gravitational field on the other hand seems to do something else other than effect the dimension that is accelerated in the line of travel. Gravitons as particles that form the shape of a gravitational field effect all three spatial dimensions simultaneously. There is a compressing of matter as multi infinite dimensions, by the gravity of matter in an increasingly more powerful gravitational field. Matter that is slowly moved into and accelerated by the effects of a more powerful gravitational field would become physically smaller in all three spatial dimensions the further into the field the matter is moved. Matter that is accelerated by energy alone to a greater constant velocity only shortens matter in the dimension or direction of motion. Other wise the energy of motion is singular but the effects of a stronger gravitational field are multi dimensional. We as individuals can physically only do one thing at a time as the threshold of time, but many people can do many things simultaneously as the event horizon. The simultaneousness of all motion (fast and slow) coupled with the spin of all matter as expenditures of energy relative to the fabric of space as non-rotating gravitons is why we experience the passage of time. In simpler terms, non-rotating gravitons as the fabric of space are the stationary face and numbers of a clock. The motions of matter including the spin of particles are the hands of the clock. Einstein used this in the "Theories of Relativity" only he termed the speed of light constant. Non rotating gravitons as the fabric of space are the carriers of all of the "Electromagnetic Spectrum". All of the electromagnetic spectrum are gravity waves. There speed, as the speed of light is constant.

The phrase, a "Gravitational sphere of perception" has already been presented although not explained. In order to explain the meaning of the phrase, a "Gravitational sphere of perception", we will view a model train on its track going around and round the track. We look at the train, and the movement of the train is in our frame of time and dimension. We take a full size-moving photo of the train going around and round it's track and contract everything in the moving photo by a ratio or scale of five to one. We now see two views of the train. One is in our "Gravitational sphere of perception", and the other is in the smaller one-fifth scale. Both of the trains are still moving at the same speed (time). Both of the trains will make one complete trip around the track together and at the same time but everything in the second moving photo is one fifth smaller.

Our "Gravitational sphere of perception" is a measurement of dimension and time as a "Graviton" (Photon, gravaphoton), as one tiny little sphere of energy of all the spheres of energy that constitute the fabric of what we call space for the entire Cosmos. (This is a Photon, and is the unite of measurement as a quanta used in Quantum electro dynamics QED) We will call this sphere of energy, dimension G (Which is a Graviton or gravaphoton). We will contract this sphere of energy (dimension G) and an area of the fabric of space where the second train is by a factor of say five to one. Although it may be three, four, up to a hundred, a thousand to one, maybe even more, maybe even up to a million to one. We will now call the contracted dimension G (Graviton), dimension M (magnetic particle). We take the moving photo of the model train, make everything in the photo into a second real model train at a one fifth scale. We contract the fabric of space as (Gravitons) of everything in the moving photo of the second model train from dimension G, (Gravitons) to the gravitationally contracted dimension M. (Magnetic particles) This contracts the substance of, and changes the frame of time and dimension of the three spatial dimensions of everything in the area of the fabric of space of the second model train. The model train at the one fifth scale, will now slow down and take maybe as much as five times as long to make one trip around the track as the train in our "Gravitational sphere of perception" which is dimension G. It takes the second model train in dimension M, as long to transit dimension M as the fabric of space for that dimension, as it does the first train to transit dimension G as the fabric of space for dimension G. Time and dimension are the same for all "Gravitational spheres of perception", (This is a postulate of the "Theories of Relativity" that the laws of nature are the same for all reference frames) but are different for differential "Gravitational spheres of perception". (The theories of relativity view this as the differential relative position and view of two or more observers) The thing is, we are in dimension G and see the second train that is in dimension M as if it were in dimension G when it is in dimension M. Because of this we see the second train run slower. The second train is now in a gravitationally contracted different frame of time and dimension than we are. This is not length contraction and time dilation as put forth in the "Special theory of Relativity". This is length contraction, "dimension compression", and time dilation that can only take place in a more powerful gravitationally contracted field.

The only difference here is that a "Gravitational sphere of perception" sees dimension contraction, and time dilation as the physical expansion and contraction of gravitational particles. Where as the "General theory of Relativity" describes this as a curve or geometric shape of the fabric of space that results in the dilation of time and the contraction of dimension and yet Einstein never really gave the fabric of space any physical substance. He simply implied that space was warped into the shape of a "Gravitational field" by the presence of mass or energy but it was still essentially space.

A difficulty in understanding the structure of a "Theory of Everything" is the fact that some of the existing theories as supporting theories are not complete. "QCD" which is short for "Quantum Chromodynamics", is a section, or part of nuclear theory that is part of the "Standard Model". The "Standard Model" is a big improvement over what they had before the "Standard Model" was put together but the "Standard Model" is still not complete. There were so many particles discovered before the "Standard Model" was formulated (over four hundred) that physicists called them the "Particle zoo". It has been determined sense then that many of the particles of the "Particle zoo" that had been discovered had different names and many were actually the same particle. Particles were named Quarks in an effort to simplify the system and it has been determined now that there are six Quarks and six leptons as fundamental particles that make up the "Standard Model" of nuclear physics.

Spin is determined in nuclear physics by using the following rule. When a moving particle is spinning to the left or to the right if the fingers of the left or right hand point in the direction of spin, the thumb is pointed in the direction that the particle is moving. Our existence is spin orientated as matter. The principle of physics presented in section two termed "Dominate Spin Rotational Orientation", simply states that there are two axis of rotation or spins found in nature as orientated to each other. This is spin to the right, or spin to the left when there are two axis of rotation present. One spin will become dominate over the other as either matter or anti-matter. A single spinning axis of rotation by itself can spin either to the right or to the left as orientated to an observer. This has been demonstrated by showing that when the axis of rotation is inverted as orientated, spin to the right then becomes spin to the left. The pole or end of the axis of rotation can also be viewed as orientated. One end of the axis of rotation as viewed is turning clockwise and the other end is turning counterclockwise. (This is the same as viewing the front and the back of a perfectly symmetrical clock) When an axis of rotation is viewed in space with no other orientation, it is impossible to tell which direction the axis of rotation is turning except as orientated to the observer. This is in a parallel with the "Theories of Relativity" that state that the observation of one observer to another is different and yet the observations of both observers are correct.

This means that when there are two axis of rotation present, there are four spin orientations for the two axis of rotation. An "Electron is spin orientated either to the right or to the left as orientated to a positron yet you can flip an electron over and it has the same spin as a positron. You can also flip a positron over and it has the same spin as an electron so which way are they spinning. It is impossible to tell with out a means of designating a spin.

The spin of an electron is designated and determined by the electron's spin of its magnetic particle's orientation to a "Graviton" as a unidirectional non-rotating particle of the fabric of space and the polarity of the flow of its magnetic particles. The super-string as a sphere of energy that is going through the ellipse, sphere, oblate spheroid cycle is spinning either to the right or to the left as orientated to a "Graviton" as a particle of the fabric of space. If the spin is to the right for an electron and it's magnetic particles to the north, then the spin of a positron as orientated to a "Graviton" as a particle of the fabric of space is to the left with it's magnetic particles also to the north. This may sound rather simple, but believe me it is not. It is extremely important. Spin has been a major problem for a nuclear physicist to determine. They are looking for an invisible arrow or signpost that will designate the orientation of the spin of "Quarks". A Graviton as a non-rotating primordial particle of the fabric of space, is that signpost and designates an orientation to the spin of particles.

Quantum nuclear theories (QCD) are built on the standard model of six Quarks and six Leptons. In the identification of Quarks, a system of colors has been used. Other names of quarks have also been used more or less at the whim of the person or persons that made the particle discovery. Quarks always come in two's and three's. Quarks and anti-Quarks are nothing more that Electrons and Positrons strung together as the nucleus of atomic particles. There is something else present that transforms them giving them a much greater mass value when they are in the atomic nucleus functioning as quarks. Before we can show how they gain so much mass as quarks, we have to present the possible spin orientations as electrons and positrons that they would have as quarks and anti-quarks when in the atomic nucleus. We will then show how electrons and positrons are changed and gain the added mass that they have as quarks and anti-quarks.

Place two positrons with an electron in between as strings or super strings as quarks as sphere's of energy that are going through the ellipse, sphere, oblate spheroid spinning cycle as presented in the presentation of an electron or positron. The two positrons are rotating one way in the same direction with the dominate electron in between rotating in the other. By inversion of the particles there are then four orientations of spin of the particles to each other. A tiny little sphere of energy, as a string or super-string as a quark, when in the cycle as an ellipse, sphere, oblate spheroid, when in the cycle as a sphere can invert as orientated to the other two quarks rotations. When in that part of the cycle as a sphere, a sphere can roll around in any direction as a sphere. An electron as a string as a cycling sphere of energy when inverted as a sphere then starts the cycle through the ellipse, sphere, oblate spheroid again. The sphere can also change polarity in that the particle not only when inverted changes rotation with out changing rotation, but rotation of the magnetic particles is reversed. When this happens, the particle completely changes rotational orientation with out ever stopping its rotation. The electron not only reverse's rotation by inversion as orientated to the other particles, but by reversal of the spin of its magnetic particles, the electron has not only changed rotation, but has completely changed magnetic polarity and becomes a positron. A positron as a quark or super string as a tiny little sphere of energy as orientated can also reverse magnetic polarity in the same manor and become and electron.

"Dominate Spin Rotational Orientation" as a principle of physics as two spins as orientated are four, and the reversal of polarity of an electron to a positron and of a positron to an electron equals as orientated six spin combinations from the two axis of rotation. There are six quarks in the standard model of nuclear physics. The six spin combinations as presented by the principle of physics introduced as "Dominate spin rotational orientation" would be the six quarks of the standard model of nuclear physics. Any of the six "Quarks" can become any of the other five and any of the six spin orientations can become any of the other five. The spin of an electron is the dominate-spin as matter orientated, and when paired with two subordinate spin orientated positrons as three quarks, is the structure of a Proton or a Neutron. Protons and Neutrons are the building blocks of the elements as matter.

The other problem is the calculation of mass. If electrons and positrons are quarks and anti-quarks, how do they gain so much mass when they are strung together as strings of matter in the atomic nucleus? There is a wide disparity of mass values that are found for atomic and sub atomic particles. The problem here is under standing what happens to electrons and positrons that changes there mass values making them into quarks and anti-quarks when they are in the atomic nucleus. The answer to this is simply that physicists do not include gravity in their calculations of mass for atomic particles. The only proven door to understanding time and dimension are the "Theories of Relativity". Einstein opened the door by formulating the theories but they are formulated for the Macro world and not the Micro. When a contracting Graviton is entered into the macro world as the fabric of space and the shape of a gravitational field, then it also will work in the micro world as a particle.

Interpretation of the "General theory of Relativity and the Sir Isaac Newton idea of interpreting gravity as an attracting force is just exactly backwards to what it means and is saying. It becomes apparent then that it is "Matter" and the "Big Bang" pressure of expansion as a force of compression that is pushing everything together. It is matter that is contracting the "Gravitational Aether" and not gravity contracting Matter. If you look at the "General theory of Relativity" in the right context, this is what it is saying. It says that the presence of mass or energy warp of curve the fabric of space. The fabric of space as a cosmic sea of gravitons is warped or curved by matter and energy into the shape of a gravitational field. Once a graviton is introduced and is seen as a particle of gravity of the gravitational aether, it becomes apparent then that it is matter that is contracting the "Gravitational Aether" as the fabric of space and not gravity contracting matter. Once this is understood it also become apparent that there is no such thing in Physics or nature as an attracting force. Particles of anything as an attracting force are a physical impossibility. An attracting force is an illusion like a flat earth or the earth as the center of the universe.

There are only three true fields, and the gravitational quantitative substance that is a "Black Hole" that are found in nature. These are a "Gravitational field", a "Magnetic field", and the "Gluon fields" found in the atomic nucleus. Each field as Gravitons (G), Magnetic particles (M), and we will call the particles that make up the gluon fields found in the atomic nucleus (E) for electro weak force, make up what has been termed three of the "Gravitational Spheres of Perception". Each particle and each field is in a different frame of time and dimension. The first one is what we view as space but is not. The second is what we view as matter and the third is what we view as the electro weak force. There is also a forth and an entirely different effect and type of field for a "Black Hole" that will be taken up in section nine. The "Gravitational Aether" as a medium that is the fabric of space, "Electro Magnetic" fields, "Gluon fields, and the substance that make up a "Black Hole" are all composed of the same particles only the particles are all in a different state of contraction.

Mass is a measure of the force that is needed to over come the resistance of matter to motion that is encountered by the coupling of matter to the "Gravitational Aether" by the explosive expansive pressure of the "Big Bang" again as a force of compression. Everything as primordial spherical particles are all geared solidly together by the "Big Bang" pressure and all particles will physically contract and roll using contraction of the fabric of space as a means of motion through the medium. It takes energy to overcome the resistance and contract and roll matter into a greater relative motion and it takes energy as resistance to overcome and reduce the greater contracting rolling motion. All the known laws of physics regarding motion, time, and inertia are exactly the same except in the understanding that all matter is solidly geared to the fabric of space by the "Big Bang "pressure of expansion. The expanding force of compression of the medium is the link between matter and the "Gravitational Aether" and is the force that matter experiences as inertia.

When energy as a singular force as motion is invoked, a super-string as a sphere of energy that is going through the ellipse, sphere, oblate spheroid cycle as an electron or positron that is solidly geared to the fabric of space has to increase or reduce its resonate rotational frequency. It increases or reduces its resonate rotational frequency by the amount of force invoked. The electron or positron as a super string is contracting gravitons to magnetic particles to match the singular motion as it physically contracts the medium. This allows the electron or positron to physically move through the medium leaving a trail of expanding magnetic particles behind it. The forced movement increases the "resonate rotational frequency" of the super string (electron or positron) and the rotational frequency of all of the magnetic particles of the magnetic field of the super-string. Everything is solidly geared together by the "Expansive Pressure" and force of compression, even the magnetic and gravitational particles as the fields of an electron or positron are geared to particles of the fabric of space. Because of this then the slightest micro movement of an electron or the expanding pressure of a single "Photon" will change the energy value of an electron. Photon energy is required to view an electron, but even the expanding contracting energy of a single photon will change the electrons energy state.

The structure of an electron or positron with their magnetic and gravitational fields has already been presented as similar to a string or super-string as presented in string theory, but instead is a tiny little sphere of energy that goes through the spinning ellipse, sphere, oblate spheroid cycle. Electrons and positrons as Leptons (as a super string) are the fundamentals of the mechanism of gravitational contraction that is the first stage of gravitational "Aether interphase" that contracts particles to the second "Gravitational Sphere of Perception". The three types of neutrinos and their anti-particles as "Leptons" are the second stage of gravitational "Aether interphase" as a devise of contraction that contracts magnetic particles to the third "Gravitational sphere of perception".

Earlier a model train was used to illustrate the changes in time and dimension between the "Gravitational Spheres of Perception". (These are the fabric of space—G, matter-M, electro-weak force- E and black hole- B). Each is like a uniform plane or plateau where particles of gravity are contracted and then held in a state of "Gravitational Aether Interphase" by the pressure of the medium, the particles spin, and the medium as a force of compression. Each "Gravitational Sphere of Perception" can be viewed as a plane or plateau with the shape of the fields (gravitational, magnetic, and gluon field) acting like funnels contracting or tapering inward to the next.

The "Electro Weak Force" does not obey parity. Parity is viewed in physics as the symmetry or equality between the left and right rotations. The principle of Physics introduced and termed "Dominate spin rotational orientation" simply states that there are two equal spins found in nature as orientated to each other and that one spin will dominate over the other as either the structure of matter or anti-matter. The dominance of the electron as matter orientated polarizes all magnetic fields found in matter out side of the atomic nucleus as spin orientated to the electron in that all magnetic particles of the fields rotate in the same rotational sequence. Evidence for this was presented by the turning of charged particles at right angles with in a Magnetic field into a circular path with in the field.

There are two wave functions that directly effect matter. The first is apparent as the "Electro Magnetic Spectrum" and the motion of Photons that has already been presented by the author.

This wave function (light) effects the first "Gravitational Sphere of Perception" as a Graviton (G). This wave function has already been presented as activating electrons and positrons as strings or super-strings as particles of matter. (This happens in a photoelectric cell, solar panels and in the operation of a CCD camera with no deterioration of the metal)

The second wave functions are waves as sound and ultrasonic sound. This wave function effects the second "Gravitational Sphere of Perception" as particle (M) magnetic particles as particles of matter. There has to be matter as a medium for the propagation of sound or ultra-sonic sound waves to take place. There is no propagation of sound waves in a vacuum. This wave function, (sound, and ultra sonic sound waves) will activate magnetic particles (M) under certain condition and then transcend them into the same spinning ellipse, sphere, oblate spheroid cycle that formed electron and positrons. The difference is that at this stage of contraction they form neutrinos, anti-neutrinos, and "Gluon" pairs found in the atomic nucleus. There will be a specific frequency or combination of frequencies of sound and or ultra-sonic sound the will activate magnetic particles as neutrinos and or anti-neutrinos under certain conditions. When a neutrino and an anti-neutrino form in the atomic nucleus they function as a pair of "Gluons". When they form out side of the atomic nucleus they function as neutrinos and anti-neutrinos. When they form inside the atomic nucleus as gluons, they can not be removed from the nucleus without them and the whole nucleus being destroyed. This will be made clear shortly when an explanation is given as to what the strong nuclear force is.

Start with two pairs of gluons, one pair of gluons with one gluon spinning right, and the other gluon spinning left. The second pair of gluons with one gluon spinning left, and the other gluon spinning right equals four gluons as orientated to the six "Quarks" of the standard model. Both pairs of gluons as orientated when they are inverted equals four more gluons. This equals eight gluons. There are eight "Gluons" in the standard model of Quantum Chromodynamics. When all conditions are right and they are activated, they will fuse particles. This starts with the production of electron positron pairs activated from an energy source. At one million electron volts, "Gamma Rays" form electron positron pairs that promptly annihilate each other. If the reactionary area where the electron positron pairs form is radiated with just the right frequency or frequencies of ultra-sonic sound waves, "Protons" and "Neutrons" will form. When formed in the atomic nucleus of an element, a neutrino and an anti-neutrino mesh as two gears spinning into each other and function as a pair of gluons. When a neutrino and an anti-neutrino are activated as a pair of gluons in the atomic nucleus of an element, they have great resistance to the pressures of motion. If a single gluon forms out side of the atomic nucleus, it is a free neutrino or anti-neutrino similar in many respects to a free electron or positron only it is at the much greater contracted state of the second stage of "Gravitational Aether interphase".

This gives neutrinos and antineutrinos tremendous leverage over electrons and positrons when they are in the atomic nucleus functioning as gluon pairs. The electro weak force has been unjustly named as the weak force. The electro weak force is the second stage of "Gravitational Aether interphase" that contracts magnetic particles (M), to gluon field particles E, and the third "Gravitational sphere of perception". Like the illustration of the two model trains that are in different frames of time and dimension, dimension at the electro weak force has been radically contracted and time has slowed down to a crawl. This gives the illusion of the "Electro weak force" as being weak and slow when it really is not. The slowness of the electro weak force could be compared to a big truck pulling up a steep grade. The transfer case is in low range and the gearbox of the truck is clear down in grandma (the lowest possible gear). The truck is moving at about four or five miles an hour pulling one hundred thousand lbs. of dead weight up a steep hill. From a distance the slow moving truck would look slow and weak compared to a truck that is speeding along on the interstate at seventy-five miles per hour. The slowness of the "Electro weak" force is an illusion created by the dilation or slowing of time and the gravitational contraction of dimension. This demonstrates the great power and leverage of the "Electro weak" force.

The "Higgs particle" as put forth in the unification of the "Electro dynamic" and the "Electro weak" forces then are gravitational particles as the "Gravitational Aether" or as a cosmic sea. The contraction of gravitational particles to magnetic particles and the contraction of magnetic particles to particles that make up the "Gluon fields" found in the atomic nucleus of the elements is the mechanism that gives electrons and positrons as quarks and anti-quarks there greater mass. There is no broken symmetry, but there are gravitational particles. It is the compression of particles to a more contracted dimension and the dilation or slowing of time as a result of that particle compression that is the mechanism that provides the greater resistance as inertial mass for the W-, the W+, and the W/o particles and not broken symmetry. Super Symmetry then is contraction of the field particles to the three gravitational spheres of perception and the contraction and singular spin of all particles of the fabric of space in the same rotational sequence that will then become a "Black Hole".

A "Muon" is a heavy electron or positron that has a measured mass value of about 200 to 250 times that of an electron. Say a Muon is two electrons with an anti-neutrino in between and all are structured to the fabric of space as has been previously presented. The anti-neutrino in between is functioning as a single "Gluon" in that it is not paired as "Gluons" are in the standard model. (In the standard model of nuclear physics, all gluons are in pairs and are the carriers of the strong nuclear force in the atomic nucleus). This "Gluon" is a "Lepton Gluon" in that it is a single neutrino or anti neutrino, and that its spin and its gluon field particles are all spinning in the same rotational sequence. This single spin "Lepton Gluon" forms a single spin gluon field that holds the two electrons together as a "Muon" until they decay or simply come apart.

The resistance to motion (inertial mass) of the large gears as the two electrons, have to over come the resistance of the smaller more contracted gears of the anti-neutrino functioning as a Gluon. This includes all particles that form the single spin gluon field that have leverage over the larger particles that are all geared to particles that make up the fabric of space (gravitons, photons or gravaphotons) into motion. Matter literally contracts and rolls through the fabric of space by contracting particles of the medium to a smaller frame of dimension and time. This gives a neutrino as a (gluon) and it's field of gluon field particles, great braking power over the two electrons. This great breaking power gives an explanation as to the "Muon" and its much greater mass value over that of a single electron.

The mass value of a "Tau" has been calculated at about 3500 times that of an electron. Again the structured is as a "Muon" only this time it is three electrons in a string coupled with several neutrinos or anti-neutrinos functioning as gluons at the poles in the magnetic fields of the electrons. Because of the much greater mass of a "Tau", there could be a pair maybe two pairs of gluons in a differential rotational sequence between the electrons. This would be a right and a left rotational pair of gluons spinning into each other which is the carrier of the strong nuclear force as presented by the "Standard Model". This is in direct conflict with the standard model that states that leptons are not affected by the strong nuclear force. Whatever the arrangement as either single spin (lepton) or dual spin (Hadron) gluons, it would give a great deal of resistance to motion. This would give an explanation as to why a "Tau" has so much more mass than either an "Electron" or a "Muon".

A "Proton" has a measured mass value of about 1,836 to 2000 times that of an electron. With this in mind, place two positrons with an electron in between as a string as a tiny little sphere of energy going through the ellipse sphere oblate spheroid cycle with their magnetic and gravitational fields all together as particles. Couple them by magnetic particles of the magnetic fields resonating as gluons pairs with their gluon fields as particles. (Again this is the strong nuclear force as presented by the standard model and this was presented in the section on Quarks) In this structure there are the two positrons with the electron in between, and all three are going through the same spinning ellipse, sphere, oblate-spheroid cycle forming their magnetic and gravitational fields, all as particles. The two positrons are rotating together in one direction and the electron as the “Dominate Spin” of matter is in between rotating in the other. Then there are the pairs of magnetic particles that are at one of the poles of the two positrons and the electron as gluon pairs. (Again the standard model calls for eight gluons) These are also cycling in the same spinning ellipse, sphere, oblate-spheroid cycle forming the gluon fields as particles, only they are in the second level of “Gravitational Aether interphase” and the third “Gravitational sphere of perception”. It can be seen in this assembly, that here is a structure that has literally millions and perhaps even billions, maybe even trillions, of gravitational, magnetic, and gluon field particles, all solidly geared to the fabric of space by the immense pressure of the “Big Bang” and the force of compression of the medium. The structure of a “Proton” has been determined to appear grainy in some tests and the complex spin of nucleons has been a problem for nuclear physicists. But then the “Standard model” of nuclear physics has not been able to include gravity or particles of gravity as part of the calculations.

The structure of a “Proton” as two positrons with an electron in between would have the positive rotation of the positrons balanced to the negative rotation of the single dominate spin electron. This would give the “Proton” a positive rotation as an electrical charge, which it does. This spin arrangement as particles, all solidly geared to particles of the fabric of space would have much greater resistance to a measured impact as inertial mass, than the single spin of an electron or a positron.

Angular momentum and a force of compression have already been discussed earlier. A skater spins with her arms out stretched, pulls them in over her head (force of compression) and gains the energy of her faster moving arms being pulled in to a shorter radius which increases her spin. This is the weak single spin torque of Leptons as electrons or positrons spinning either to the right or to the left. Now take two skaters, one spinning to the right and the other spinning to the left. The two spinning skaters, one to the right and the other to the left can catch a third skater in-between and send the third skater flying clear across the ice and still retain there position in the arena. They have the balanced power of dual spin or the opposing rotations of angular momentum.

What this illustration shows is the weaker leverages of either the right or left-hand single spin of "Leptons" as compared to the much greater power of dual or opposing spin leverages of "Nucleons" or "Hadrons". The right and left-hand spin of a proton or a neutron geared solidly to the fabric of space greatly increases the resistance to impact that is manifested as increased inertial mass. This coupled with the contracted rotational leverages as braking power of neutrinos and anti-neutrinos functioning as gluons in the atomic nucleus, would give a clearer understanding as to why the proton has such a much greater measured mass value over the mass of an electron or a positron.

Understanding these spin relationships and the power of the greater leverages of contracted particles as aspects of "Gravitational Aether Interphase" coupled with "Dominate spin rotational orientation" as two principles of Physics, the rest of the elements can be assembled as the structure of matter. The structure of matter it will be found is simply electrons and positrons as quarks and anti-quarks or strings and super-strings coupled together with neutrinos or anti-neutrinos (as gluons) into strings and loops that form the nucleus of the elements with one spin dominate over the other. The dominate spin either to the right or to the left as orientated, will determine if the structure of existence is as matter or as anti-matter. In the case of our existence, the spin of an "Electron" and not the "Positron" is dominate as matter. Only electrons and not positrons form in the "photo-electric" effect, "solar panels", and in the operation of a

"CCD camera" and the human race is predominately right handed. Anti-matter is of course structured exactly backwards to matter.

This then if proven correct, unifies three of the four forces as one. The first three are the contractions of gravitational particles (photons or gravaphotons) as particles of the fabric of space by the two stages of "Gravitational Aether interphase" disclosing three of the four "Gravitational spheres of perception. From there, there is another mechanism that completes the contraction of gravitational particles to the quantitative substance that is the essence of a "Black Hole".

The fourth force, the strong Nuclear force is manifested as the dual explosive expansion at the speed of light of all the particles that make up the entire atomic nucleus. All particles are solidly geared together by the expansive explosive force of the "Big Bang" and under a force of compression of the medium. Magnetic particles, gluon pairs, and gluon field particles, as contracted particles are all under the powerful tension of contraction to explosively expand. They are held in their contracted state by the spinning vortex action of angular momentum under the expansive explosive force of compression of the "big Bang". The strong nuclear force is released when the atomic nucleus is broken. When the atomic nucleus is broken, pairs of "Gluons" that are spinning as the true right and left hand rotation of electrons and positrons spinning into each other as two meshing gears, LOCK with a third non-rotating particle (graviton, gravaphoton) of the fabric of space. When they LOCK with a third non-rotating particle, all particles of the atomic nucleus that are solidly geared to each other, immediately lose their spin and explosively expand. They expand with a sudden violent explosive snap at the speed of light as the expansive cycle of all wavelengths of the "Electro Magnetic spectrum". (This again is the expanding cycle of a photon as a wave of the electro magnetic spectrum as presented by the author). For there to be this release of energy, (the strong nuclear force), there always has to be the spin of two particles from both rotations spinning into each other like two meshing gears. (The true right and left hand spinning particles LOCK with a third non-rotating particle of the fabric of space).

All "Magnetic fields" out side of the atomic nucleus as the dominate spin of our orientation and existence as matter, are single spin "Magnetic fields". In magnetic fields as matter orientated, all the magnetic particles of magnetic fields spin in the same rotational sequence. The release of all conventional forms of energy (everything) other than nuclear are the expansion of single spin "Magnetic particles" orientated as the spin of matter.

When an electron and a positron come together in a particle accelerator, they promptly destroy each other. The magnetic particles of the magnetic fields of an "Electron" and a "Positron" are spin orientated exactly backward to each other. If they can come together with no non-spinning particles of the fabric of space in between they will mesh like two gears, one turning right and the other turning left. Positrons and electrons as particles are arranged like this in the atomic nucleus where all particles are running smoothly spinning into one another as the structure of matter. When they are free electrons and positrons in the "Gravitational Aether" and come together, the magnetic particles of the magnetic fields will "Lock" with a third particle of the fabric of space in between. (Again this is a graviton, photon or call it a gravaphoton) When they LOCK, they immediately loose there spin and expand with the same sudden violent explosive snap as a release of the strong nuclear force that was presented earlier when the atomic nucleus of a heavy element was broken.

If it were possible to produce a bar of anti-iron and place it in the vicinity of a bar of matter iron. Induce electromagnetic induction in both bars by winding a coil of insulated wire around each of the bars, both bars would destroy each other in a burst of pure energy that was just presented when an electron and a positron collide in a particle accelerator. The opposing right and left hand spinning "Magnetic particles" of the electrically induced "Magnetic fields" of both bars would LOCK with a single non rotating neutral black Photon, (Gravaphoton) as a particle of the fabric space between them. When they LOCK it would cancel out the spin of all the "Magnetic particles" that make up the "Magnetic fields" of the two bars. The LOCKED" "Magnetic particles" of both of the electrically induced "Magnetic fields" would then expand with the same sudden powerful explosive expanding snap at the speed of light as the expanding cycle of photons. This is a release of the strong nuclear force in the fission cycle. When the electrically induced "Magnetic fields" were destroyed (converted to energy) the "Magnetic fields" of the iron and anti-iron atoms themselves would also LOCK and be destroyed. This sequence of events would result in a complete and massive conversion of matter to energy.

Using the principle of Physics termed "DOMIMATE SPIN ROTATIONAL ORIENTATION" it again becomes apparent that the formation of matter as matter or anti-matter is determined by the dominance of one spin over the other. This is either dominate spin as orientated to the right, or dominate spin as orientated to the left. Again in the case of our existence, there are simply more right handed people in the human race than there are left.

SECTION—6

It is a mandate of the "Theories of Relativity" that the speed of light is constant for all frames of reference or inertial systems regardless of their differential relative velocities to each other. On the other hand, the "Electromagnetic Spectrum" experiences the Doppler shift of light spectra in a similar manor as sound waves do in the atmosphere. This is what destroyed the "luminiferous Aether" theory back in the nineteenth century. It was expected that the "luminiferous Aether" was similar to the atmosphere and that the propagation of light as of the "luminiferous Aether" would be similar. Physicists tried experiment after experiment with an instrument called an optical interferometer to try and find a relative motion of the earth to the speed of light and of course they failed in their attempts.

The spin structure, of an electron and a positron have already been presented. Using the two principles of physics that were introduced has brought an understanding to the mass of subatomic particles and has provided a structure for matter and a means of unifying the four forces of nature. All atomic particles are formed as a "magnetic dipole" in that they have a semi-closed "magnetic field" that has a north and a south pole of the particle. This allows some of the magnetic particles of the dipole-pole magnetic field that are ejected perpendicular to the pole and the particle, to break free of the particles magnetic and gravitational fields. These magnetic particles then form what is known as a "Mono-pole" magnetic field. A "Mono-pole" (singular) magnetic field is a magnetic field that has no polarity as north or south and does not cycle in a field as a dipole-pole magnetic field does. This magnetic field is charged or energized by the escaping magnetic particles from all the dipole magnetic particles that are the quantitative substance of the celestial sphere and of all matter.

Magnetic particles that build up in matter as a "Mono-pole" magnetic field, will then be ejected straight out from matter in all possible physical directions in straight line's relative to that matter. When the quantitative substance as matter forms a mass that becomes great enough that a "celestial sphere" forms, "Mono-pole" magnetic particles are then ejected as infinite radii of a sphere. Again this is straight out and in straight lines from the sphere relative to the sphere. This is the hidden symmetrical magnetic field that contracts the "Gravitational Aether" into the symmetrical shape of a gravitational field for matter. The principles and structure of "Gravitational Aether interphase" as a system of gravitational contraction of gravitational particles has already been presented. The only difference is in the magnetic fields. The type of field for particles of matter and for matter in motion, as was shown by the structure of an electron or positron is curved by the contraction of gravitational particles of the gravitational field. Magnetic particles have their trajectory bent by the contraction of gravitational particles around and then back into a vortex and through matter with a north and a south pole. Magnetic particles in a dipole type magnetic field continually cycle as a partially closed system that allows magnetic particles that cycle perpendicular to the escaping pole (probably the north) to escape the system.

A "Mono-pole" magnetic field, that contracts a gravitational field, is also a closed magnetic field system but there is a difference. Magnetic particles that become a "Mono-pole" magnetic field first contract the fabric of space into the shape of a gravitational field by "Gravitational Aether interphase". This happens when monopole magnetic particles pass between non-rotating particles of the fabric of space as gravitons. With their greater rotational leverage, they impart a partial or fractional rotation of particles of the fabric of space all in the same rotational sequence. Non-rotating particles of the "Gravitational Aether" as (Gravitons, photons, gravaphotons) forced to turn all in the same rotational sequence by the greater leverage of the more contracted mono-pole magnetic particles, interfere with each other and they contract. Mono-pole magnetic particles on their way outward from matter to the outer most fringes of the gravitational field, "Interphase" in between particles of the fabric of space and in doing so, contract these gravitational particles as "Gravitons" that are on their way to the celestial sphere as contracting "Graviton motion". This two-way motion of mono-pole magnetic particles outward from matter and gravitational particles contracting inward into matter, warps or curves the fabric of space into the shape of a gravitational field as described by Einstein in the "General Theory of Relativity". "Mono-pole magnetic" particles after reaching the extremities of the gravitational field, expand back into full sized "Gravitons" as particles of the fabric of space and then may return to be contracted by more magnetic particles, again as part of the gravitational field. This then is a tri-stage or three phase continual motion of particles as the cycle of gravitational and monopole magnetic fields.

Most of the magnetic fields that are detected by science are dipole (two pole) magnetic fields and all magnetic particles orientated as matter, rotate in the same direction as orientated. The sun has two magnetic fields. The first is apparent and is due to the rotation of the sun and is a "Dipole" magnetic field similar to the "Dipole" magnetic field of the Earth, Jupiter, Mars, and any body that rotates. This magnetic field forms because of the additional motion as rotation of the object and because particles of the object are at a higher energy state as motion ejecting these motion induced magnetic particles that form the dipole magnetic field. (There is a third magnetic phenomena for the sun that has to do with the sun's "sun spots". This can not be presented now because we are not ready for the presentation but it will be presented later). The suns second and hidden "Mono-pole" magnetic field that shapes the suns gravitational field, is the force that forms and has been detected as the solar wind. The solar wind is a consequence of the "Mono-pole magnetic field" of the sun. The solar wind was not known about until mankind ventured into the vacuum of space beyond our atmosphere and it was then discovered. The solar wind is an effect of the mono-pole magnetic field propagated outward from the sun in all directions in straight lines giving a symmetrical shape to the gravitational field of the sun. The solar wind as a "Mono-pole magnetic field" carries small bits and pieces of matter (electrons, protons, neutrons, helium nuclei, etc) that are drawn together by their own gravitational fields of contraction and are carried out to the extremities of the suns gravitational field. Here they form as dirty balls of the lighter gaseous elements that make up the composition of comets and may eventually return to the sun, carried there by the contractual "Graviton motion" of gravitational particles as the gravitational field of the sun. It will be found that all of the planets will have a magnetic wind that is the "Mono-pole magnetic field" of the planet.

The "Mono-pole" magnetic field has a uniform rate of motion as monopole magnetic particles moving out of a celestial sphere anywhere from the surface of the sphere that curves the fabric of space into the shape of the gravitational field. This changes the physical dimension of the fabric of space. When physical dimension changes, time is different for differential dimensions. This rate of monopole magnetic particle motion is added to the motion of the celestial sphere as it transits the fabric of space as a medium. The two velocities are added together in the line of travel and subtracted in the line away from travel. This is exactly the same thing as if you were traveling in a car, and fired a bullet from a gun in the same direction that the car is moving. You would add the velocity of the car and the bullet together. (Light is different) If you were in the same car and fired the gun back behind the car you would subtract the velocity of the car from the velocity of the bullet. If there were many guns firing all around the car from the car and in different directions, the bullets would all be at a uniform distance from the car no matter how fast or slow the car was traveling. This allows mono-pole magnetic particles that form the "Mono-pole" magnetic field to be at a uniform distance from the celestial sphere regardless of the spheres relative velocity to any other sphere. The mono-pole magnetic field then contracts the "Gravitational Aether" into the shape of a gravitational field that is moving with the celestial spheres regardless of the differential relative velocity of the celestial sphere to any other celestial sphere. Any frequency of the electro magnetic spectrum that enters the contractual moving gravitational field of the celestial sphere will then be propagated at a uniform speed from any direction of the celestial sphere. The spectra of light will be red or blue shifted in direct proportion to the strength of the gravitational field and position of the observer. All extraterrestrial light that reaches our planet, is blue shifted by the Gravitational field of the earth and all light from out side of our solar system is blue shifted by the Gravitational field of the sun. Gravitational red and blue shift of the spectra of moving celestial objects is an observed and calculated science. All celestial spheres have a gravitational red shift of the spectrum that can be interpreted as the mass of the object.

Einstein simply said that the speed of light was constant for all reference frames of inertia regardless of the differential relative velocities to each other but could give no reason for the consistency. It turns out that he was right anyway. He spent the last thirty years of his life tying to unify the fields. The trouble was, he was trying geometrically to unify a "Magnetic Dipole" as a magnetic field to the geometric shape of a gravitational field as put forth by the "General theory of relativity". This can not be done. The magnetic field that will unify the fields is a "Magnetic mono-pole". Back when Einstein formulated the "Theories of Relativity", the electro weak force had not yet been discovered. Neither had the solar wind. Understanding both of these phenomena would have been tremendous help in trying to unify the fields. In understanding the relation ship in unifying a Dipole magnetic field, with a "Mono-pole" magnetic field and a gravitational field, finally bridges the great chasm that has existed between the "Theories of Relativity" and "Quantum theories". The "General theory of Relativity" as a "Macro" field theory, will unify with a "Mono-pole" magnetic field as a "Macro Magnetic" field. "Quantum theories" and a "Dipole magnetic" field are already unified as a "Micro magnetic" field theory. Unifying a dipole magnetic field and a “Mono-pole” magnetic field will then unify “Quantum theories” with the “Theories of Relativity”.

It turns out that Einstein and Physicists of the nineteenth century were both right to a certain extent. The composition and motion of the “Mono-pole” magnetic field that forms a gravitational field were not understood back in the nineteenth century. Because of this the “Luminiferous Aether” as a theory was laid to rest. Now understanding that the consistent motion of the fields with and as part of all reference frames are responsible for the consistency of the speed of light for the reference frames, a modified “Luminiferous Aether” theory then again becomes tenable. Inertial systems moving at a relative velocity to any other inertial system radiating frequencies of the “Electro Magnetic Spectrum”, experience the Doppler shift of the “Electro Magnetic Spectrum” similar to sound waves in the atmosphere. This means that the constant speed of light is dictated by a constant medium in space out side of a gravitational and magnetic field. That medium, is the “Gravitational Aether” under the explosive expansive pressure of the “Big Bang”.

SECTION—7

When a thermonuclear reaction is brought about, a nuclear device is exploded first to provide heat to trigger the event. This is about ten million degrees Celsius. This involves bombarding about thirty lbs. of Uranium two thirty five as a critical mass or about five lbs. of Plutonium two thirty nine as a critical mass, with neutrons. The neutrons change some of the nuclei to Uranium two thirty six in one reaction and Plutonium two forty in the other both of which are highly unstable. In using either reaction, the result is a breaking of the nucleus in a violent chain reaction that escalates rapidly into a nuclear explosion. The nuclear explosion provides heat that triggers the fusion of hydrogen to helium with a subsequent release of a very large amount of energy. This sequence of events is a brief description of the steps taken to bring about a thermonuclear reaction.

The structure and cycle of a typical wavelength of the "Electro Magnetic Spectrum" as presented by the author, has already been covered in previous sections in this discussion. Because this structure shows so much about the expansion and contraction of the medium as the common denominator that unifies the four forces, it is going to be partially presented again to show it's relation ship to a "Thermonuclear reaction".

Around an energy source, a spherical shell of particles of the fabric of space (gravitons, gravaphotons) expand as the beginning of a wavelength of light and are detected as "Photons" of the "Electro magnetic spectrum". A second spherical shell of particles as a band outside the first expanding band, remains black and neutral but moves in-concert away from the first expanding band as the moving band to make room for the first expanding band. A third spherical band as a shell of particles outside the second moving band, contracts to make room for the moving band. The first expanding band is the FISSION cycle as expanding photons as a release of energy and the third contracting BLACK band is the FUSSION cycle of "Photons" as the contracting cycle of waves of the "Electro magnetic Spectrum". In other words in alternating between the two as a wave function, the expanding cycle as photons is FISSION and the contracting cycle as the black body effect is FUSION.

When the "Thermonuclear reaction" that fuses hydrogen as an element to helium as a heavier element takes place, there is a contraction of particles of the fabric of space at the speed of light that become particles of the fields and of the atomic nucleus. To give an exact placement of the contraction and identify each particle is not only in practicable but very likely impossible. The complex grainy structure of a proton has already been presented, so trying to identify all the particles would be something like trying to identify every particle of sand in a whole truckload. There would be literally millions and perhaps even billions and even trillions of particles of the fabric of space as "Gravitational, Magnetic and Gluon field particles" that contract for the structure of each atom. When the contraction of particles of the medium is made to form the heavier element, the contraction that happens again at the speed of light, opens a multi-dimensional hole in the reactionary area of the "Gravitational Aether". All individual particles of the fabric of space (gravitons, gravaphotons) as the quantitative substance that is the "Gravitational Aether", are under the explosive expansive pressure of the "Big Bang" to expand but are contained by the presence of the medium as a force of compression. When the multi-dimensional hole is opened by the mass contraction of particles to fuse the heavier element, all particles that constitute the quantitative substance that is the "Gravitational Aether", expand en-mass as one giant expansion of particles of the fabric of space. In the "Thermonuclear" release of energy, every individual photon, (graviton, gravaphoton) that make up the entire substance of the medium as the fabric of space of the reactionary area, expands with a sudden powerful expanding snap as the explosive expansive power of the "Big Bang". This explosive expansion is again at the speed of light, and is the expansive reaction of X to the x power of trillions of particles that close the multi-dimensional hole. The explosive energy of this "big Bang" expansion focuses in and on to the newly fused Helium and then rebounds as the thermonuclear shock wave. The rebounding thermonuclear shock wave is an extremely powerful massive series of gravitational waves that physically move, distort and displace the fabric of space as the fission expanding and fusion contracting cycle at all frequencies of the "Electromagnetic Spectrum".

This is the "Thermonuclear reaction", and it is the source of energy when Hydrogen is fused to helium and to a lesser degree all of the heavier elements that are fused to the complexity of the iron fifty-six atomic nucleus. This release of energy is similar to the release of energy that takes place when a fission nuclear bomb is detonated, only this release of energy is by expansion of all particles of the medium and is on a much more powerful, and intense scale. The difference is that in fission, the particles are already in a contracted state as part of the atomic nucleus. When the atomic nucleus is broken and they enter the fabric of free space, they "LOCK" with a third NON-rotating particle of the fabric of space (Graviton) and expand with a sudden violent explosive snap at the speed of light as a release as the strong nuclear force. Where as the thermonuclear release of energy is an expansion of all individual particles of the entire fabric of space in the reactionary area due to the contraction of particles of the fabric of space fusing the heavier element.

The explosive expansive "Big Bang" power of the fabric of space as the "Thermonuclear reaction" that has just been presented, coupled with the expansive action of the "Magnetic Mono-pole" as the stars secondary magnetic field, is what makes a star shine. If the mass of the celestial sphere is great enough, the contractual motion of gravitons, (gravaphotons) as particles that form the "Gravitational field" of the body will be moving so fast toward the body that they escape the confining force of compression of the medium. The fusion of Hydrogen to Helium is deep within a star that is in a main fusion sequence. The contraction at the speed of light of particles to form the heavier element that has just been presented, keeps open a depression or hole in the fabric of space inside the star. This in effect lowers the expansive pressure of the "Gravitational Aether" below the expansive pressure of the "Big Bang". This allows expansion of Photons as (Gravaphotons) as expansive thermonuclear energy during the contracting "Graviton motion" cycle of gravitational particles into the star before they ever enter the star.

As an example of this, the visible surface of the sun is at about 6,000 degrees Kelvin and the chromosphere, which extends out several thousand kilometers is at about 30,000 degrees Kelvin. The "Corona", which extends clear out into inter-planetary space has a temperature of about 1,000,000 degrees Kelvin. What the mechanism is that heats the sun's "Corona" so hot has been a major problem for Astro-Physicists to explain. In understanding the thermonuclear reaction that has just been presented, the answer to this becomes obvious. The suns "Corona" is hotter and shines because of the explosive expansive "Big Bang" thermonuclear reaction of photons (gravitons, gravaphotons) of the "Gravitational Aether" as photon expansion. This expansion is toward the hole in the fabric of space that is inside the star. There is a mass expansion of gravitational particles (gravitons, gravaphotons) as thermonuclear energy in space around the sun before they ever enter the sun as particles of gravity. This coupled with a partial expansion of the suns "Mono-pole magnetic field" that creates the sun's solar wind is what makes the sun and all stars shine and is the sun's corona.

SECTION—8

The formation of the elements listed on the periodic table start with the main sequence in the life of a star and this is the fusion of hydrogen to helium. This is followed by the fusion of Carbon, Neon, Magnesium, Silicon, Chromium, and finally elemental Iron if the star is large enough. Iron fifty-six has been termed the deep valley of the elements and is the final formation in this stage of fusion. A super giant star will fuse iron in and as its central core. It is believed that the lighter elements are layered around the iron core in spherical shells with the heavier elements deep within the star. During this sequence of fusion some of the elements of the periodic table in the stars layered shells have not been fused and none of the heavy elements from iron to the uranium group have formed.

Some astronomers and Astro-physicists in trying to understand the explosive mechanisms of type two super-nova, have theorized that after the Iron core has formed and at a critical period, the Iron core suddenly collapses to the density of and forms a Neutron star as the central core of the star. The resulting inward collapse of the shell of lighter elements then impacts the super dense Neutron star and rebounds as the mechanism that blows the star apart as a type two super-nova.

Fusion as has been presented, is the conversion or contracting of energy to matter. Matter is contracted energy in a passive state. This involves the contraction of particles of the fabric of space by the two stages of "Gravitational Aether interphase", to three of the four "Gravitational spheres of perception" that has already been presented. To fuse the heavier elements from Iron to Uranium, there has to form a condition that would be best termed as "INTER-MAGNETIC SPACE". Do not confuse this with a "Magnetic field". "Inter-Magnetic space" is not a "Magnetic field" and has no resemblance what so ever to what we view as space or a "Magnetic field" of any kind.

There are twenty-six chemical elements plus their isotopes from hydrogen one to iron fifty-six with hydrogen as by far the most abundant. There are sixty-six chemical elements plus their isotopes and this is not counting the heavier ones fused artificially in the laboratory, from iron fifty-six to uranium two thirty eight, the heaviest element found in nature. These heavier elements are among all the rare earths and precious metals that are found in very small amounts.

They have had trouble with computer models showing the lighter shell elements of the star imploding when the neutron star forms and then rebounding as a device that would generate enough energy to blow a star apart as a type two Super-nova. The implosion of the shell elements, and then the shell elements rebounding at impact from the surface of the "Neutron star" just does not generate enough energy to blow a star apart. On top of this, the "Gravitational field" of a "Neutron star" would be so intense and powerful that anything that imploded that short of a distance to the surface of the "Neutron star" could not possibly rebound and escape anyway. Instead the material would be smashed flat, bound to the star's surface by its super powerful gravitational field. Also, this sequence of events does not really account for all the stages of nuclear fusion that is central to the formation of all the elements. All of the elements exist and there has to be a way for them to form. There are the lighter elements that were skipped in the outer shells of the star during the initial stages of fusing to the star's core of Iron fifty-six and then all of the elements with a greater atomic number than iron fifty-six on the periodic table. This is the entire list of heavy elements plus their isotopes from iron fifty-six to the uranium group and then those that have been created artificially in the laboratory.

There have been developed by some Astrophysicists and Astronomers, additional involved complicated round about theories detailing fusion of the heavy elements, but these theories just do not provide satisfactory answers to all of the questions regarding fusion in a straight forward, rational manor. Once the fusion of elemental Iron has formed in a super giant star there is a barrier to the fusion of heavier more complex elements found on the periodic table. In current nuclear theories, the barrier is because it seems to require more energy than is released in order for more complex elements to fuse. Iron, as an element does not want to react to either fusion of fission. There has to be a change in conditions after the formation of the iron core in order to continue the fusion of Iron to the heavier elements and it is not just the star blowing its self-apart that does it. All the elements from Iron to the uranium group on the periodic table are heavier nuclei consisting of more and more neutrons and protons that are increasingly more complex and unstable. Iron is the fundamental element. All of the elements, light, and heavy pivot around iron. Iron in a solid metallic state is readily magnetic up to the "Curie" point. Iron as the core of a super giant star is in a condition or state as metallic plasma.

When the fusion of Hydrogen to Helium as the main sequence of the star nears completion and Iron has fused as a core in the star, three distinct changes or conditions in the star start to take place. One, the quantitative "Mono-pole Magnetic field" of the star increases due to the tapering off of the main sequence of fusion. Two, NON-ROTATING "Magnetic particles" as an inter-neutral pole of the Mono-pole magnetic field, start accumulating in side the Iron core of the star as a sphere of what has been presented as "inter-Magnetic space". And three the intensity of the "Gravitational field" as the actual contracting motion of "Gravitons" into the star is diminished due to the tapering off of the main sequence of fusion. (Gravitons as particles of the fabric of space, contract during fusion to heavier elements. This was presented in section seven as the thermonuclear reaction. Partial completion of fusion lessens the demand for the contraction of gravitational particles as graviton motion. The reduction or lessening of graviton motion contracting into the star is a weaker gravitational field).

Now as was said, do not confuse "inter-Magnetic space" with a "Dipole Magnetic field" (duality), a mono-pole magnetic field (singular), or any magnetic field of any kind. The "Mono-pole Magnetic field" is in interphase out side of the star, and is the mechanism that contracts gravitons as the fabric of space into the shape of the "Gravitational field" of the star and has already been presented. All atomic particles as the quantitative substance and mass of the star are dipole magnetic, and if the star is rotating, form a vortex magnetic field that is propagated through and then pole to pole of the star. This magnetic field is curved into a vortex by the contraction of gravitational particles into the celestial sphere in exactly the same way that the "Gravitational and Magnetic" fields of an electron or positron were that was presented earlier in the text.

In side the Iron core of the star; NON-ROTATING "Magnetic particles" are accumulating into a sphere in what has been termed "inter-Magnetic space". It is the first contracted level of "Gravitational Aether interphase inter-space" and it is very hard, dense, and extremely heavy. Nothing known to man is as hard or dense. None of the known elements can even begin to penetrate it. In this medium (inter-Magnetic space) neutrinos and anti-neutrinos (Or as gluons) as sympathetic resonating "Magnetic particle Super-Strings" can physically move. They are the only things in existence that can. There are no electrons, positrons, mesons, protons, neutrons etc. inside the sphere of "Inter-Magnetic Space". These can exist on the surface of the sphere connected as strings or super-strings and in the form of neutrons, but not inside the sphere it's self. There are no frequencies of the "Electro magnetic spectrum" that can even begin to penetrate or effect "Inter-Magnetic Space". Even the highest frequency X or Gamma rays can not penetrate this medium. The reason for this is that there simply are no particles of the fabric of space (photons as gravaphotons) to resonate any frequencies of the "Electro Magnetic spectrum" with. They have all been contracted to the dimensional state and dilated time frame as NON-ROTATING magnetic particles. The only waves as energy in existence that can effect "Inter-Magnetic Space" are sound and or ultra-sonic sound waves.

When the "Mono-pole Magnetic field" of the star increases, and "Graviton motion" as the contracting movement of the Gravitational field decreases (Gravity weakens) the whole star expands or swells as a result. "Magnetic particles" as "Inter-Magnetic Space" in their neutral NON-spinning state are under internal pressure of each particle to explosively expand as the fission cycle of the strong nuclear force. (The expansion cycle as waves of the electro magnetic spectrum). This is manifested as an explosive expansive pressure of the sphere of "Inter-Magnetic Space" to explode within the iron core. The contained explosive expansive internal pressure of the sphere of "Inter-Magnetic Space" would result in the iron core and the whole star expanding. As the star expands, the sphere of "Inter-Magnetic Space" as the internal expanding force, in expanding is weakened by the increase to a greater volume. The "Gravitational field" at greater diameters then again gains dominance and the star will contract. This sets up a cycle in that the star will oscillate, balancing between the explosive internal expansive pressure of the sphere of "Inter-Magnetic Space" to explode, and then rebounding in a contracting cycle when the "Graviton motion" of gravitational particles at greater diameters again gains dominance. (Gravity)

The cycle of expanding, contracting oscillations of the star would produce what would be best termed as massive star quakes, only of an immense magnitude that would make our earth quakes pale as nothing by comparison. Some stars as super giants expand and contract to extensive radical extremes. As an example, if the red super giant Betelgeuse were where our sun is, its contracted diameter would expand from about the dimensions of the orbit of Mars or less out to somewhere beyond the orbit of Jupiter when expanded and back again. It continually flickers and seems to cycle in about a fourteen-month period.

The Illustration of a skater that spins with her arms out stretched and then brings them in over her head, which increases the spin of her body, again shows the effects of angular momentum. To induce angular momentum, there always has to be a force of compression first. This force of compression for the skater is the energy that it takes for her to pull her arms in over her head to a smaller radius of rotation. Her arms at the greater radius are traveling faster and when pulled into the smaller radius, the energy of her faster moving arms is transmitter to her body and she spins.

"Inter-Magnetic Space" is confined as a sphere within a core of Iron, which is a medium that is in a state as metallic plasma with in the star. The massive star quakes as a result of the cycle of oscillations would produce frequencies of sound, both audio and ultra sonic that would resonate with the expanding contracting cycles of the star and the iron core. Both audio and ultra- sonic frequencies of sound produced as a result of the star quakes are waves of energy, that would react at a critical frequency and be instrumental in the energizing of "Magnetic particles" as Neutrinos and or anti-Neutrinos. (Or as gluons)

As the expanding contracting cycle of oscillations of the star compress and expand the iron core and the sphere of NON-rotating "Magnetic particles" as "Inter-Magnetic Space", a shell of rotating "Magnetic particles" form on the surface of the sphere of "Inter-Magnetic Space". The film of rotating "Magnetic particles" is between the sphere of "Inter-Magnetic Space" and the iron core. With each cycle of expansion and contraction, the sphere of "Inter-Magnetic Space" starts to rotate, dictated by the "Dominate spin rotational orientation" of the star and under the powerful gravitational and inertial compressing force of angular momentum riding on the shell of rotating "Magnetic particles". The rotational frequency of the sphere of "Inter-Magnetic Space", increases with every cycle of expansion and compression of the star. With each compression cycle of the star, rotating "Magnetic particles" of the rotating magnetic shell are bombarded by frequencies of sound both audio and ultrasonic from the massive star quakes. This coupled with the powerful inertial driving force of compression to angular momentum, energize "Magnetic particles" as Neutrinos (Or as gluons) that are driven inward into the sphere of "Inter-Magnetic

Space" and outward into the stars iron core. (Earlier it was stated that there would be specific frequencies of sound either audio or ultra-sonic or a combination of these frequencies that would activate "magnetic particles" as neutrinos, anti-neutrinos, and gluons).

Neutrinos and anti-neutrinos (Or as gluons) driven into the sphere of "Inter-Magnetic Space" invoke a contracting caving in motion of non-rotating "Magnetic particles" of the medium in exactly the same manor as electrons and positrons do in what we perceive as the fabric of outer space (gravitons) that has already been presented. Each Neutrino or anti-neutrino functioning as a lepton, (single) or Hadron, (double) gluon pair, forms gluon fields that have rotational dimensional leverage over and contracts non-rotating "Magnetic particles" of the fabric of "Inter-Magnetic Space" into "Gluon field particles". Each neutrino (Gluon) contracts a tiny area of the sphere of "Inter-Magnetic Space", reducing some of its dimensional volume as non-rotating "Magnetic particles" to rotating gluon field particles and elevates some of the explosive expansive pressure to explode. This contracting power of Neutrinos (Gluons) helps to contain the explosive expansive power of the sphere of "Inter-Magnetic Space" and stabilizes the cycle of oscillations of the star. The star will then stabilize as a super giant.

From the fields of rotating gluon field particles, NON-ROTATING "Gluon field particles", collect in the core of "Inter-Magnetic Space" as "Gluon field particle inter-inter-space" in a similar manor that NON-rotating "Magnetic particles" collected in the Iron core and formed the sphere of "Inter-Magnetic Space". If the star is of sufficient quantitative mass, a "Black Hole" will start to form in the NON-rotating core of "Gluon field particle inter-inter-space ". If a hole starts to form, the star is doomed. The whole mass of the star will contract until it becomes part of the growing "Hole".

The Mechanism that forms the "Hole" is the dominate rotational spin of the star its self which is super imposed as spin to the sphere of "Inter-Magnetic Space" and accelerated by the repeated oscillations of the star. The repeated oscillations of compression and angular momentum augment and multiply the spin of the sphere of "Inter-Magnetic Space" for each oscillation, and it will reach great cycles of rotational velocity. This is how a neutron star reaches such fantastically high revolutions of rotation. The internal neutron star is rotating and increasing its rotational frequency in synchronization to the expanding and contracting cycles of the star long before the super giant as a star ever explodes.

Gravitational particles (gravitons, gravaphotons) that have been contracted to the rotational dimensional mass as the substance of Gluon fields and Gluon field particle inter-inter-space are almost pure passive inertial energy in a contracted state with little or no dimensional mass. With such a minutely small dimensionally contracted mass, the super-accelerated dominate spin of the sphere of "Inter-Magnetic Space" would be sufficient to spin these particles all in the same rotational sequence. When particles all spin in the SAME rotational sequence, they interfere with each other and they contract. This would take place at the axis of rotation of the sphere. Here the rapidly spinning sphere of "Inter-Magnetic Space" has the greatest leverage and power. Here the accelerated rotation and leverage of the sphere of "Inter-Magnetic Space" (the neutron star) is great enough to spin "Gluon field particles" as "NON-rotating gluon field particle space" (inter-inter-space) all in the same rotational sequence. This is the final contraction to the fourth "Gravitational sphere of perception" that is the quantitative substance of a "Black Hole". Physical dimension as a diameter and spin of the newly forming "Hole" is there, but there is no possible way that this can be detected or measured, and time as we know it for the singularity internally has stopped. A "Black Hole" does not experience time. To experience time, there has to be a beginning and an end of an expenditure of energy or dimensions. Internally in side a "Black Hole", time and dimension are zero as there is only one motion and this is spin either to the right, or spin to the left as the dominate spin of the "HOLE". There is no simultaneousness of motion to the right and motion to the left to measure as the passage of time.

When Neutrinos and anti-neutrinos (As gluons) are driven into the sphere of "Inter-Magnetic Space" from the shell of rotating "Magnetic particles", each powerful compressing cycling oscillation of the star also drives them outward into the Iron core. Neutrinos and anti neutrinos (As gluons) driven outward into the Iron core by the cycling oscillations of the star, invoke fusion of the Iron atoms to the rest of the heavy elements with each cycle of contraction and compression. The repeated stellar contractions invoke pressures of inertial compression and angular momentum that far exceed the force of normal static contractions of gravity for the mass of the star. This powerful force of inertial compression is the mechanism that fuses the rest of the heavy elements. They fuse from the inside of the Iron core out. They layer out in thin shells around the sphere of rotating "Inter-Magnetic Space", fused from the Iron.

First a shell of cobalt forms, then Nickel followed by copper, Zinc, Gallium, Arsenic, and so on until all of the heavy Elements of the periodic table have formed inside the Iron core and out side of the sphere of "Inter-Magnetic Space". This is a second stage of nuclear fusion that takes place after Iron fifth six has fused as the central core of the star. This second stage of nuclear fusion takes place after a star has become a super giant, and is cycling through the expanding contracting oscillations of angular momentum and as the main fusion of Hydrogen to Helium nears completion. In the fusion of more complex elements, more complex elements hold larger more complex electron shells, which increases electron pressure with in the iron core of the star. Increased electron pressure expands the Iron core, which increases the stability of the star although the star will expand some more and become a larger super giant.

If the star is of a sufficient quantitative mass as a super giant, all known elements fuse clear up to and including the uranium isotopes. It has been said that plutonium can not exist in nature, that it is man made. It is my belief that anything that man can do, can and does happen in nature, even so if plutonium did not form, uranium two thirty five would. How much uranium two thirty five would it take to blow a star apart when it reached a certain stage and then started to fuse to uranium two thirty six? Thirty pounds is a critical mass for a nuclear bomb. How many trillions of tons of uranium two thirty five would exist inside a super giant star? If the star is large enough, when the uranium two thirty five in it's core begins to fuse to uranium two thirty six, it starts to explode as a type two Super-nova.

The initial or first stage of the exploding star, is a super-giant fission nuclear bomb of magnanimous proportions. Neutrinos (Gluons) at the on set of the explosion would be driven from the rotating "Magnetic shell" through the Iron and spherical layered lighter elements at or very near the speed of light. The flood of Neutrinos (Gluons) passing through the Iron core, and then through the layer of lighter elements of the stars shell, would ignite a thermonuclear reaction in these layered lighter elements that finishes blowing the star apart as a type two Super-nova. If there were not sufficient Neutrinos and anti-neutrinos (As gluons) in the sphere of "Inter-Magnetic Space" forming a massive gluon field for the sphere that holds it together, the sphere of "Inter-Magnetic Space" itself will also explode as part of the super nova.

The variables of different super-nova then are what does a star have left for an outer shell of the lighter elements when it explodes. Does it still have Hydrogen left as a shell, or has the hydrogen mostly fused to helium? Maybe the helium has mostly fused to carbon and the star going super-nova is a carbon star! Does the sphere of "Inter-Magnetic Space", explode as part of the super nova, or is it left as a Neutron star as in some cases? Different types of supernova would be directly related to what the star had left for lighter elements as a shell after fusion when the star explodes. A type one super-nova would be a super giant star that has no lighter elements as a shell to ignite as the thermonuclear reaction. This super-nova would be strictly and explosive nuclear reaction device. The detonation of an exploding star as a type two super-nova, is about the same thing that takes place when mankind explodes a nuclear device first that triggers the detonation of a thermonuclear or Hydrogen bomb. This then is the mechanism that forms the Neutron star that is sometimes left over after a super giant star explodes as a type two super-nova and not the contraction of Gravity as put forth in current theories. The Neutron star is a sphere of "Inter-Magnetic Space" saturated with Neutrinos functioning as hadron gluon pairs and lepton gluons forming gluon fields into one super massive nucleus that keeps the neutron star from exploding.

The gravitational field of a Neutron star that did not explode as part of the super-nova, is a two-stage mechanism of contraction and it is the only gravitational field of its type in the Cosmos. Again do not lose sight of and the perspective that it is the incredible explosive expansive pressure of a "Bang" or the "Big Bang" as the fabric of space that is pushing everything together as a force of compression. This force of compression and the contracting compressing vortex action of particle spin is what holds everything together. This collapse of the force of compression due to the vortex action of spin and angular momentum, pushes everything in existence together clear right down to the quantitative substance that is the essence of a "Black Hole".

Neutrinos and anti-neutrinos, as "Lepton gluons" and "Hadron gluons" are the second stage of "Gravitational Aether Interphase Inter-Magnetic Space". The structure here is exactly the same as the structure that was presented as the fabric of outer space with electrons and positrons as the contractual device, contracting "Gravitons" (Photons gravaphotons) G, to magnetic particles M. A "Neutron star" is a sphere of inter-magnetic space held together by a massive gluon field. This is the main substance of the neutron star and what the star is made of. Neutrinos (Gluons) are the primary devise of contraction of a "Neutron star" and would build a massive "Gluon field" around the surface of the star of "Gluon field" particles. Because of the stars high rate of spin, the star builds a dipole “Gluon field” that cycles through the star around the surface and back to the stars other pole similar to the Magnetic field of a rotating star or planet. The difference is that the dipole “Gluon field” is at the second stage of “Gravitational Aether interphase”. The “Gluon field” on the surface of the star is stretched flat to the surface binding the shell of rotating “Magnetic particles” to the star.

Particles of the fabric of space, (gravitons, gravaphotons) pushed to the surface of the star by the “Big Bang” expansive pressure, are contracted by rotating “Magnetic particles” of the shell of rotating “Magnetic particles”. They are then contracted again by rotating “Gluon field particles” and become part of the gluon field as gluon field particles. This forms an intense dual combination “Magnetic particle and Gluon particle field” that sharply contracts and curves the “Gravitational Aether” into a very steep powerful gravitational field for the star.

The flow of dipole gluon field particles cycles from pole to pole and then through the star like a high powered miniature dipole magnetic field only this field is composed of gluon field particles and is stretched flat to the surface of the star. At the exit pole, (North Pole) particles of the dipole system as gluon field particles escape and exist from the star. They expand back to magnetic particles and then back to “Gravitons” (Photons, gravaphotons) that resonate as “Electromagnetic radiation”. This “Electromagnetic radiation” has been detected as a highly uniform precise signal that is in tune with the rapid rotation of the star and the stars have been called pulsars. (The first pulsars were detected by an under-graduate student named “Jocelyn Bell” in November 1967)

Our sun and solar system are believed to have condensed from the remnants of a “Supernova”, the explosion of a super giant star. Scientists base their beliefs in part on the presence of heavy elements in the earth and in the spectral analysis of the sun. The sun contains heavy metals including Iron. The tiny planet Mercury is believed to be almost a solid block of iron. The Earth and Venus are believed to contain large iron cores.

Jupiter is believed to have some iron in its core. It has been determined that Mars also contains much iron. Many of the asteroids and meteorites are iron and nickel iron. Because of this, you could take the position, that a super giant star that had an iron-core and exploded as a super-nova and then condenses into our sun and planetary system, that our sun would have to have iron as a core. Now I do not mean especially a large core or that it fused there, of course not. The sun is too small to fuse iron, but the iron would have fused in the formation of the super giant star that exploded and condensed to our sun and planetary system.

There is an anomaly to the sun, the anomaly is the sunspots that periodically appear for a while and then disappear. Some of them are large enough to hold several of our earths and they are known to effect radio and television transmission. They also effect the weather here on earth and have been determined to be powerfully magnetic in nature. This then could be construed as to be the partial formation of "inter-Magnetic space" that formed in a small iron core with in the sun. The quantitative mass of the sun is not great enough to contain "inter-Magnetic space" with in an iron core that did not fuse there, so it periodically bubbles to the surface as the sunspots that we detect and observe.

Depending on the size of the star, giant, or super-giant and the amount of uranium fused in its core, the star could start to explode and then contract again. It could do this over and over again expanding and contracting in a cycle until it eventually explodes or else the uranium in the core breaks up into lighter elements and the star goes into a state of equilibrium. If the star is smaller, about the size of our sun, then the powerful contracting action of Neutrinos functioning as Gluons and the great rotational leverage of Gluon fields will eventually contract the star to the density of a white dwarf. If the star is larger but of a size that sufficient elements of the uranium isotopes do not form in its core to make it explode as a supernova, then the star will go into a state of equilibrium. The star will burn through both hydrogen as the first and iron as the second stages of fusion and build a huge single spin "Mono-pole Magnetic field" that will repel other stars of the same Dominate spin. Old red stars, estimated to be anywhere from seven to twelve or thirteen billion years old, collect around the cores of Galaxies and into Globular clusters. They exist in Globular clusters because of the massive single spin "Mono-pole Magnetic fields" they have that repel each other almost as strongly as the "Graviton motion" of particles of gravity into the stars carries them together. The older a star of a sufficient mass becomes, the slower is its rate of fusion, and fusion may cease all together as the star stabilizes. When this happens, the stars "Mono-pole Magnetic field" becomes very large, powerful, and intense. This is the repulsion of single spin "Magnetic particles" and is electron pressure only on a stellar magnitude. A star does not have to be under going fusion in order for the star to shine and radiate frequencies of the "Electro magnetic spectrum". Just the "Graviton motion" as gravity of particles of space into a star of sufficient mass as the maintenance of stable matter (mostly iron) would be great enough to invoke expansion of the fabric of space as thermonuclear energy before the motion of Gravitons as gravity ever enters the star. This was shown in section seven.

Globular star clusters are also contracting to a singularity as a "Black hole". Old stars with their huge "Mono-pole Magnetic fields" in congregating into a globular cluster would have the "Mono-pole Magnetic field" of the cluster at a much greater intensity deep with in the cluster. The deeper into a globular star cluster a star is the stronger will be the "Mono-pole Magnetic field" of the cluster that the star is in. The "Mono-pole Magnetic field" of a globular cluster will increase in intensity until a sphere of "inter-Magnetic space" is encountered as a core of the cluster. When old stars in the core of a globular cluster collide, merge or fuse into a single super giant star, the intense "Magnetic fields" of the stars of the globular cluster would contain the explosive expansive pressure of a sphere of "Inter-Magnetic Space". The same sequence of events (compression, angular momentum and the mechanisms of contraction) that formed a "Black Hole" in the core of a Neutron star when it is in the core of a super giant star, are taking place in the core of a globular cluster. The difference here is that there is no fusion of heavy elements taking place that would blow the globular cluster a part as a "Super Super-Super-Supernova". A globular cluster will eventually form and become a massive "Black Hole" that is a singularity as the seed of a Galaxy.

When matter is accelerated to the speed of light, there are two reactions that take place. The reason that matter can not exceed the speed of light is apparent as the structure of a photon of the "Gravitational Aether". A Photon (Gravaphoton) as a sphere of energy can not expand and contract any faster forming waves of the "Electro magnetic spectrum". This is a fixed speed limit of expansion and contraction as a reaction that is built into Photons (gravaphotons) as the fabric of space. When matter is accelerated to the speed of light, all components as super-strings would revert back to and become a wave function of the "Electro magnetic spectrum". The energy of the wave then re-forms as particles of matter. Accelerated particles of matter can not travel at the speed of light, but waves of the "Electro magnetic spectrum" can, so the particles revert back to waves of the "Electro magnetic spectrum" again. This sets up an alternating wave particle function in that the energy is first in the form of a wave, and then as particles of matter, then as a wave, then as particles of matter and so on. This alternating energy wave matter sequence, is the structure of the propagation of radioactive radiation and high-energy particles known as radioactive fallout.

On the other hand, cosmic rays or cosmic radiation produce particle energies that are mind boggling. The energies of cosmic rays that have been measured far exceed anything that mankind can achieve in even the most powerful particle accelerator to date. When the supernova of 1987 in one of the Magellanic clouds was observed, neutrinos were detected before visible light. This has been interpreted to mean that neutrinos are capable of exceeding the speed of light. It has also been shown by the structure of the theory outlined in this manuscript how neutrinos can exceed the speed of light if there is a means of accelerating them. Magnetic fields can not accelerate Neutrinos beyond the speed of light but if there were a way of using the energy of Gluon fields found in the atomic nucleus, this might be accomplished. A neutrino accelerated to ten times the speed of light would have tremendous energy. A Neutrino accelerated to one hundred times the speed of light or more would have a catastrophic effect when it collided with any particle of matter. This raises the possibility that the phenomenon of cosmic radiation that has been detected at high altitudes in the atmosphere are indeed neutrinos or antineutrinos that have been accelerated to multiples of the speed of light. There were no cosmic radiation detectors in place like the fly's eye previous to the 1987 supernova in one of the Magellanic clouds that would have detected a flood of cosmic radiation from the supernova. Because of the time frame, the relativistic effects of particles at extreme velocities, and the uncertainty of the true velocity of the particles at these velocities, (say neutrinos at ten times the speed of light) a time of arrival would be impossible to predict. Cosmic radiation from the event could have arrived anywhere from minutes, a year to perhaps several thousands of years before visible light actual arrived that would then confirmed the transition of the event. Because of the possibility of super accelerated neutrinos or anti-neutrinos (faster than the speed of light) as the mechanism responsible for cosmic radiation, the origin of cosmic radiation may be impossible to detect with present day science.

SECTION—9

Again because of its importance, the principle of physics that has been introduced and termed "DOMINATE SPIN ROTATIONAL ORIENTATION" that was previously presented is being presented here again in the section on Galaxies.

If we take just the hands and the face of a clock with out the body of the clock and make them symmetrical in every way, (no numbers or distinguishing markings) it would be impossible to tell which way the clock was running except as orientated to the observer. If we view the clock from one side face on, the hands are turning clockwise, view the clock from the back of this side, and the clock is turning counter clockwise. Because of this it would be impossible to tell if the clock were running clockwise or counter-clockwise except as orientated to the observer. In effect the same motion of the clock is running both clockwise and counter clockwise at the same time. If we remove the hands and the face of the clock and leave just the axis of rotation and view this from edge on, the axis of rotation becomes a cylinder. We draw a perfectly symmetrical line the length of the cylinder so we can tell if the cylinder is rotating, and if it is rotating which way is the cylinder rotating. We can invert the cylinder as orientated and like the hands of the clock the same identical spin that appeared as spinning to the right, will then be spinning to the left. You can look at a perfectly symmetrical rotating cylinder as an axis of rotation and say that it is turning right from one perspective, but from another the same identical rotation will be turning left. So which way is the cylinder turning, to the right or to the left? We can physically stop the rotation of the cylinder and as orientated, rotate the cylinder in the other direction. If we close our eyes and lose orientation, then we still have the same problem as to which way the cylinder is rotating. (The axis of rotation could be inverted or reversed when your eyes were closed and when you opened them you would not be able to tell what the rotation was except as orientated)

This is the concept of a singularity or how a duality becomes a singularity of motion. If there is introduced a second cylinder then we can tell if they are spinning in the same rotational sequence, or opposite of each other. If they appear to be spinning into each other by inverting both cylinders, the same identical spin of both cylinders will then be spinning away from each other. If we invert one of the cylinders, then they will be spinning relative to each other either to the right, or to the left. As long as the cylinders were perfectly symmetrical and indistinguishable, it would be impossible to tell which way they were rotating with out the other one as a frame of reference to orientate it to. Then all that can be told is whether they were spinning in the same or opposite rotational sequences as orientated to each other. None of the cylinders has reversed rotation at any time which shows that any single rotation, is all so a dual rotation. If one of the cylinders is larger of smaller than the other one, then they can be spin orientated relative to each other. Now if we paint a mark on one end of the cylinders white and the other end black, then we can designate one end say as white north and black as south.

A non-rotating "Graviton" as a tiny little sphere of energy would be symmetrical in every way. There would be no way of telling anything about the sphere as far as polarity goes unless there was invoked rotation of the particle. The same rules of rotation that applied to the cylinders as an axis of rotation would apply to a "Graviton" and all perfectly symmetrical particles as spheres of energy.

A "Black Hole" as a singularity of motion, the last contracted state of "Gravitational Aether interphase" and the final "Gravitational sphere of perception" has no magnetic field of any kind. The Mechanism of contraction is different than that for particles, celestial spheres, Neutron stars, and Galaxies. Like a featureless perfectly symmetrical spinning cylinder, it is a mechanism of singular directional motion. By inverting, the "Hole" as orientated, right can become left and left can become right.

The pressure of an expanding "Big Bang" or a "Bang" as particles of the fabric of space (photons, gravphotons) and strings or super-strings as particles of matter, are the mechanisms that increase the quantitative substance of a "Black Hole". A "Black Holc" as a singularity of motion has actual physical dimension but there is no direct way that it can possibly be measured. The quantitative substance of the "Hole" is the hardest material in the entire "Cosmos". The surface is also the smoothest surface in the entire "Cosmos" and the blackest black in color although the blackness of the "Hole" as a color can not be told from the blackness of the "Gravitational Aether". The "Hole" is spinning as a super vortex of motion, but because of what it is made of as the final contraction of gravity, it can not radiate or reflect any frequencies of the "Electro-magnetic spectrum". Because of this the "Hole" it's self can not be directly detected by an observer. Particles of the fabric of space, gravitons (gravaphotons) pushed to the surface of the "Hole" by the "Big Bang" expansive pressure of the medium, are all forced to spin in the SAME rotational sequence by the overpowering dominate spin of the "Hole". The SAME rotational sequence of particles of space all forced to spin in the same direction invokes rotational interference of the particles with each other and as they spin, they contract. They continue to contract until they become part of the "Hole".

With out a "Dipole, Mono-pole or any type of magnetic or Gluon field" to contract the fabric of space inward to the "Hole", a gravitational field or depression of curvature that exists around Electrons, Positrons, planets, stars and Neutron stars does not develop. As particles of the fabric of space spin and collapse into the "Hole", the fabric of space of a large area around and away from the "Hole" expands dramatically and keeps expanding as a negative gravitational field. There is nothing coming back out of the hole that is a recycling of the fabric of space as in the gravitational field of a star or planet, where the "Mono-pole" magnetic field through expansion and contraction becomes gravitons and gravitons become magnetic particles again. This produces a curvature of space and time as a gravitational field that Einstein" described in the "General theory of Relativity". That type of 'Gravitational field" is a positive or focusing "Gravitational field" in that particles of space are more contracted as they move deeper into the field.

The Gravitational field of a "Black Hole" is structured the other way around in that it is a "Negative" gravitational field. In a "Negative gravitational field", particles of gravity do not contract but instead expand as they move deeper into and approach the "Hole". This is because particles of the fabric of space are being consumed by and are becoming part of the hole but again absolutely nothing is coming out of the "Hole". This gives the illusion that the fabric of space is expanding around the hole and it is, only it is expanding and then being devoured by the hole. Any light that is propagated through the gravitational field of a "Black Hole" instead of being refracted inward as in a curved lens, that has been termed "Gravitational lensing" will be refracted outward as in a negative lens.

In the famous test that confirmed Einstein's "General theory of Relativity", during the eclipse, starlight was refracted by the suns gravity inward toward the sun by the predicted amount. In the "Gravitational field" of a "Black Hole", starlight would be refracted outward away from the Hole. This further increases the illusion that the cosmos is expanding when it is not. The "Hole" will devour the fabric of space around the "Hole" and build a huge spherical bubble of expanded and expanding space around the "Hole".

Because a "Black Hole" has no "Magnetic field", it has no inertial or gravitational mass as matter. "Inertial mass" is the result of the link of "Magnetic particles" being geared solidly to "Gravitational particles" of the "Gravitational Aether" by the explosive expansive pressure of the "Big Bang". If a "Black Hole" is in motion relative to the fabric of space or a quantitative substance as matter, there is absolutely nothing in existence that can stop its motion other than physical contact with another "Black Hole".

A "Black Hole" as a symmetrical singular contraction of Gravity is a singularity of motion, that has no right or left hand orientation. One can become the other, and the other can become the one. When two "Holes" come together it does not mater what there orientation was as left or right hand spin as matter or anti-matter when they formed, one or both will invert until one is spinning right and the other is spinning left as oriented to each other. When two "Holes" come together and have aligned, with out ever reversing their spin, they form right and left-hand orientations as dual motions to each other. The dual motions of one "Hole" to the other again with out ever reversing their basic spin, reverse the contracting action on the surfaces of both "Holes" and the surfaces start to expand. Once the surfaces start to expand the two "Holes" have ignited as a "Quasar". Once they have gone into spin reversal and ignited as a Quasar, they release incredible amounts of energy, the fabric of new space as Photons (Gravaphotons) and the orientation as duality starts to form matter.

The reaction of a pair of "Black holes" as a Quasar or multiple "Black Holes" forming multiple quasars is the engine that fuels a Galaxy. The principle of Physics that has been introduced and termed "Gravitational Aether Interphase" is in reversal here. It is simply a matter of reversing the sequence of events that led to the formation of a singularity when a "Quasar" is ignited. A "Black Hole" by its self is a singularity of motion as passive energy. It is when two of them come together and the orientation of both of them as right and left hand form a duality of motion to each other that the presence of existence, the dimensions of reality, and the passage of time is created.

The first dimensional density is that of "Gluon field particle inter-inter-space", then "inter-Magnetic space" and finally particles of the fabric of what we call space. The reaction as a reversal of the two "Holes" explosively expanding, is the fission expansion cycle as the expansive cycle of waves of the "Electro Magnetic Spectrum". (Photon expansion) Particles at the perimeter of the reaction are more expanded than particles expanding from the feature less surface. Smaller more contracted particles interphase or wedge in-between larger particles and there is a mixing or homogenizing of different dimensional densities as spherical particles of energy. When particles of Gravity had expanded sufficiently for the four "Gravitational spheres of perception" to form, (Black hole B, Electro weak E, Magnetic M, and Graviton photon G), the building expansive pressure activates Electrons, Positrons Neutrinos, and anti-Neutrinos. These four fundamental super-strings and "Magnetic particle" super-strings constitute the basic building blocks of matter. This has been gone into and their function and formation already presented in previous sections. When the formation of particles of matter begins, it partially re-contracts the expanding particles of the fabric of space and helps to reduce the expanding pressure.

None of the four basic particles can exist alone in the curvature of the other spin orientated singularity's field of expanding particles of gravity as the fabric of space. If an electron or a neutrino entered the expanding particles of Gravity of the other spins rotational orientation, it would be destroyed. The same is true of positrons and anti-neutrinos. Because of this, the particles fuse into a single particle as a neutron. A free Neutron by itself can invert or polarize relative to the motion of orientation and become a particle as either a neutron of matter, or a neutron of anti-matter. Because of this a neutron is compatible with the curvature or orientation of either spin. A neutron as matter orientated, consists of a polarized proton with an electron stuck on one end held there by a neutrino or multiple neutrinos functioning as a gluon or gluons. It is held there by its gluon field spin and the ever present pressure of the medium. If a neutron is inverted and polarized as anti-matter it becomes an anti-proton with a positron stuck on one end held there by a neutrino (Gluon). In decay it becomes and anti-proton with a positron and an anti-neutrino.

As the expansive reaction progress's, quantitative neutron mass material, builds up for both rotations. The spin of each singularity orientated to each other as either right or left hand spin induce a chirality or handedness of curvature into the quantitative neutron mass material of each singularity. The chirality then induces curvature in the neutron mass material that promotes decay of the neutrons. A neutron entering the singularity gravitationally orientated curvature as "Matter" will decay into a proton and the W minus particle. The W minus particle will then decay into an Electron and an anti-Neutrino. In the other spin orientation as anti-matter, it would be an anti-proton, and the W plus particle. The W plus particle would then decay into a positron and a neutrino. In neutron decay as matter orientated, protons released from twenty-six Neutrons and their accompanying anti-neutrinos (Gluons) would fuse with thirty neutrons into the iron nucleus. The twenty-six free electrons that were released from the neutron decay then become the electron shells of the iron Atom. In the anti-matter reaction, as spin orientated, twenty-six neutrons polarized, as anti-matter would decay into twenty-six anti-protons. There accompanying neutrinos (Gluons) would fuse with thirty inverted (polarized as anti-matter) neutrons into anti-iron. The twenty-six free positrons released by the decay would then form the positron shells of the anti-iron nuclei.

Because of the principle of physics introduced and termed "Dominate spin rotational orientation", if one of the singularities is of a greater quantitative value than the other, the greater dominate quantitative value of the one will induce subordinate spin in the lesser and it will circle the greater. This will bring the iron and anti-iron atoms of both singularities together. The iron, anti-iron atoms, and their magnetic fields as spin orientated are structured exactly backwards to each other. The iron and anti-iron atoms in coming together react in a fission sequence that was described earlier in section five as an iron, anti-iron electro magnetic induction reaction. When they come together, the conflicting right and left hand spin orientated "Magnetic particles" of the "Magnetic fields" of both the iron and anti-iron atoms LOCK with a single none rotating expanded neutral photon (Gravaphoton) as a particle of the fabric of space. When they LOCK, they expand with a sudden violent explosive snap at the speed of light as the expanding cycle as photons, (photon expansion) of the "Electro magnetic spectrum". This then induces a complete break up of the iron anti-iron's atomic structure clear right down into their smallest string or super-string components. These are (electrons, positrons, protons, anti-protons, neutrinos, anti-neutrinos, etc). The result is a massive fission (expansive) reaction of both spin-orientated materials, culminating in the core of the Galaxy exploding. In the reaction, neutrinos, anti-neutrinos, (Gluons) and particles that form the gluon fields that fused all the strings and super-strings of matter and anti-matter together, expand and become particles of the fabric of space as photons (gravaphotons). All that is left of the iron and anti-iron atoms is detected as the gas and dust clouds found only in the arms of spiral galaxies.

The arms usually form in pairs although a peculiar galaxy may have one arm. The chirality or handedness of the galaxy that is determined by the rotation of the smaller singularity around the larger forming the quasar, would align or polarize the super-strings as either matter or anti-matter. The differential quantitative value of the singularities determines the size and shape of spiral Galaxies. Two singularities of almost equal quantitative value will form a bar galaxy.

The light from all Quasars has their spectra strongly shifted to the red or long end of the spectrum. This has been interpreted as meaning that the object is receding or moving away from the viewer. When an object is moving toward the viewer, just the opposite takes place in that the spectral lines of spectra are shifted to the blue or short end of the spectrum. Astronomers and Astrophysicists can then make calculations as to the velocity that an object is receding away from, or moving towards the viewer by how much the spectral lines of a spectrum have shifted. The spectral red shifts of Quasars have been interpreted to mean that some of the objects are moving at upward to 90 percent of the speed of light away from the viewer.

As has been presented a Quasar is ignited when two or more singularities as “Black Holes” are reacting forming the core of a new Galaxy. The reaction not only creates new matter, but the “Fabric of new space” as well. This then explains the red shift of Quasars. The fabric of new space is being created by the reaction of the singularities as a Quasar. It is the fabric of new space created by the Quasar, and then being ejected from the Quasar, that is moving toward the observer at up to ninety percent of the speed of light. The fabric of new space moving toward the observer, has the same effect as if the object were moving away from the observer and would red shift the Quasars light in the same identical fashion. This then is the cause of the red shift of the spectra of quasars and galaxies and not the motion of the Quasar and Galaxies themselves. The actual relative motion of the Quasar would be very little if any relative to the “Gravitational Aether” that is at absolute rest. If it were possible to circumnavigate a Quasar, the red shift of its spectrum would be almost the same from any direction regardless of the position of the observer. The red shift of the spectra that is being interpreted as meaning a recessional velocity of the object then is an illusion created by the fabric of new space explosively expanding from the Quasar.

Understanding the loss by expansion of neutrinos and anti-neutrinos as energy during the iron anti-iron fission reaction that culminated in an explosion of the core of a spiral galaxy, gives an understanding to the mass defect curve of the elements from iron fifty six to Hydrogen one. All that would form would be iron and anti-iron if there were no reaction when the two came together. None of the lighter elements would form and we would not exist. It takes energy to fuse or restore the neutrinos and anti-neutrinos that were lost as particles of the fabric of space in the matter anti-matter (fission) reaction of the iron and anti-iron atoms. Fusion is the conversion or contraction of energy to matter, so energy is needed in order to fuse the elements and their isotopes back to the complexity of the iron fifty-six atomic nucleus.

It has been asserted that a "Graviton" and a "Photon" are the same particle and that all of the "Electro magnetic Spectrum" are Gravity waves of the "Gravitational Aerther". The waves are propagated by the expansion and contraction of the energy particles under the pressure of the "Big Bang". It was also shown how there would be a chirality or handedness to the texture of space itself. This was demonstrated by showing columns of spheres forming a six-sided geometrical figure of infinite dimension that when under a helical twist either to the right or the left became a circular column. Super-strings orientated as either matter or anti-matter are spinning to the chirality or handedness of the helical twist of the "Gravitational Aether" as it is orientated on a galactic scale of a galactic arm determined by the origins of the singularity. The iron atom is perfectly balanced to the curvature of the rotation of the singularity structured as matter orientated. Anti-iron is balanced to the other rotation of curvature as spin orientated. When the iron anti-iron reaction of the pair of singularities exploded forming the spiral arms of the galaxy, the resulting orientation of curvature as either matter or anti-matter left the lighter elements from hydrogen one to iron fifty six unbalanced to the curvature of the singularity as matter orientated.

The structure of a proton compensates for the curvature by spinning the positive subordinate spin of two positrons to the dominate negative spin of one electron. A Proton that formed from two electron positron pairs will then have the second electron in a slot like orbit making the spin as electric charge neutral. The initial spin orientation of the singularity to the galactic curve of the galactic arm as either matter orientated or anti-matter orientated is the mechanism for the excess energy of the lighter elements. This is why the proton will not decay and again the human race is predominately right handed. All the planets in the solar system spin around the sun in the same direction instead of both directions and all of the stars in a spiral galaxy rotate around the galactic core in predominately the same rotational sequence.

The same curvature of the dominate singularity as matter or antimatter as the galactic curvature of the "Gravitation Aether" is also the mechanism that unbalances the heavier elements as they fuse in the core of a super giant star. The more complex the nucleus becomes, thc more neutrons are needed to maintain the balance orientated to the curvature of the singularity as orientated as either matter or antimatter. When the complexity of the nucleus reaches the level of the uranium group, nuclei that are of odd unbalanced combinations are easily broken back into smaller more stable components with a subsequent release of a large amount of Energy.

The Gravitational field of a Galaxy is all together different than that shown for a star, a neutron star, a planet and a "Black Hole". Astronomers, Astro-physicists and Scientists have long felt that there is missing matter in the "Cosmos". Because of this, there has been a search for missing matter or dark matter as it has been called, but none has ever been found that would give a satisfactory explanation. Astronomers and asto-physicists have come up with all kinds of exotic weird involved theories trying to explain the so-called missing or dark matter. Much of the belief that there is missing matter in the cosmos and it is estimated that as much as up to 90% is missing is due to the motion of stars in the limbs of spiral "Galaxies".

Stars in the limbs of spiral galaxies all travel at the same speed regardless of their distance from the galactic core, which is contrary to what happens with planets in our solar system. Planets closer to the sun have faster orbits than planets farther out where as the stars in the limbs of spiral galaxies all move at the same speed regardless of their distance from the galactic core. Because of the stellar motion in spiral galaxies, it is believed that there should be more mass than has been accounted for although how more mass would make the stars all travel at the same speed is a very good question that would have to be answered. There are also the motions of some Galaxies them selves that cannot be accounted for by using current theories of mass and gravitation. New discoveries indicate that there are rivers of galaxies in space that are moving in the wrong direction to be compatible with a uniformly expanding cosmic scheme as professed by propionates of the current "Big Bang" theory.

The reaction of two singularities that have ignited as a quasar and gone into reversal as "Black Holes" are also releasing particles that form the new expanding fabric of space as has been shown. The spiral arms that formed in the iron anti-iron reaction not only build gas and dust clouds, but clouds of the fabric of new space as well. Each spiral Galaxy is a reacting exploding little "Big Bang" pushing expanding particles of new space and other Galaxies away from and apart by the reaction. The expanding arms are composed of the fabric of new space and spin with the spiral of the galactic core carrying the newly forming stars in the new space at the same relativity velocity. The stars are just being carried along for the ride. Using "Newtonian mechanics" and the "Theories of relativity" as a means of making calculations of stellar motions have all the stars traveling to fast in the limbs of spiral galaxies. It is the new fabric of space of the spiral arm that is spinning with the rotation of the galactic core of spiral galaxies. A spiral Galaxy is revolving like a giant Ferris wheel with the Galactic core, the fabric of new space as the arms and the stars all moving together and yet the arms are dragged back into the curved spiral by interference with the fabric of old space of the "Gravitational Aether". Our star the sun and the planetary system that we live in are in the arm of a spiral galaxy. Our motion, as part of the fabric of space of our spiral arm relative to the rest of the cosmos, will have a bearing on the analysis of the "Electro-magnetic spectrum".

The two principles of physics that have been introduced, "DOMINATE SPIN ROTATIONAL ORIENTATION" and "GRAVITATIONAL AETHER INTERPHASE" then will explain the structure of the "Galaxies". To gain an understanding of this, we will look at a few galaxies and apply the principles of physics that explained the structure of the limbs of spiral galaxies. We will also use the conclusions that were drawn from the relative speed of light as presented in section six. The conclusions provided for a "Frame of absolute rest" when there is no magnetic or gravitational field present. For those that will argue that there is no "Frame of absolute rest", it can not be gotten around that light experiences the Doppler shift of the "Electro magnetic spectrum" the same as sound waves do in the atmosphere. Because of this we can conclude then that the "Cosmos" seems to be more like a vast ocean or "Cosmic Sea" of gravitational particles with most of the fabric of space at rest and yet it expands, contracts and the Galaxies seem to be moving away from each other.

In applying the principles of physics and as an example of explaining the shape and motion of a galaxy, there is a beautiful barred spiral with the designation of NGC-1365 in the "Fornas cluster". This Galaxy was picked at random and just because there happened to be some information about it at the time. It is believed to be at a distance of about sixty million light years. The same principles presented concerning this galaxy would apply to all and any galaxy.

This galaxy is a massive bared spiral with the bar as equal arms reaching from the core opposite each other and of about equal length. It is not orientated to our field of view as flat on to us, but is more of an angle that tilts away from our position. At the ends of each arm of the bar is a large mass that is curved as a spiral that tapers down and then traces a faint circular pattern clear around the whole Galaxy. This Galaxy would have two "Singularities" as "Black Holes" of almost equal quantitative value reacting in reversal as the core of the Galaxy and ignited as a "Quasar". Quantitative value of this magnitude for this galaxy is not of absolute equal value. This has let the core engage in a very slow "Dominate spin rotationally orientated" spiral. The slow spiral has allowed the build up of a rotating sphere of the fabric of new space that was emitted from the "Quasar" that built up around the galactic core before it exploded. This sphere of the fabric of new space is rotating with and is part of the galactic core of the galaxy. When the iron and anti-iron atoms build up to a quantitative value and finally came together, they exploded and the bar started to form. The bar that started to form is then carried along with and rotates with the sphere of the fabric of new space and the galactic core of the galaxy. When the exploding bar that is rotating with the rotating sphere of the fabric of new space, reaches the extremities of the sphere of the fabric of new space, it encounters the fabric of old space that is at absolute rest as the "Gravitational Aether". The ends of the bar are then wiped off and are suspended in that part of the cosmos that is at absolute rest with the rotating "Galaxy". The ends of the bar that are wiped off into that part of the Cosmos that is at absolute rest, will continue to get larger and longer as the bar continues its explosive expansion from the galactic core. The sphere of the new fabric of space, the bar, and galactic core will continue there slow but majestic and unified progressive galactic rotation. This gives the galaxy a beautiful but fantastic shape.

In another application, the popular spiral galaxies M101 or M51 are both flowery spirals with a pair of arms that curve clear around the galactic core. Both galaxies were picked as similar but at random for presentation. This type of galaxy would have as a core, two "Black Holes" ignited and reacting in reversal as a "Quasar" with one "Hole" being of a much greater quantitative value over the other one. Again the principle of physics termed "Dominate spin rotational orientation" applies.

The extreme unbalance of the quantitative value of the reacting "Singularities" as a "Quasar" does not allow the time interval that is necessary to build a rotating sphere of the fabric of new space around the galaxy as in the bared spiral. The much smaller subordinate "Hole" in rotating much faster around the dominate "Hole" brought the iron and anti-iron atoms together much sooner and the "Galactic core" exploded right away. The fabric of new space that forms the spiral arms in exploding, encounters the "Gravitational Aether" that is at absolute rest. This curves the arm around the galaxy into its long beautiful spiral. This then is a mixing of the new fabric of space that is the spiral arms, with the "Gravitational Aether" that is the old fabric of space that is in a state of absolute rest.

"Quasars" have been detected in the galactic core of elliptical galaxies as well as in the spirals and have also been detected in what are called peculiar galaxies. The size and shape of all galaxies are determined by the quantitative value of the "Singularities" as "Black holes" that are reacting to each other forming a Quasar. There could be more than one pair of "Singularities" even three, four or maybe more in a galactic core. Multiple reacting "Black Holes" as quasars would be defined as odd shaped or peculiar galaxies. In more bizarre shapes, a Galaxy that is in motion relative to the "Gravitational Aether" that is at absolute rest would have its shape changed by that motion as well as galaxies that have come together and merged or collided. Also the fabric of new space would move the fabric of old space like ocean currents that would distort the shape of some galaxies. The motion of exploding spiral arms relative to the "Gravitational Aether" would form gravitational rip tides of changing time and dimension at the arms perimeters that would possibly be extremely dangerous to enter or pass through. A vehicle in space could be sheered into two sections by passing from the fabric of new space into the fabric of old space with no way of ever getting the sections back together.

Reacting "Black Holes" that ignite and form quasars as galactic cores would not always be easy to detect. It may be that in some galaxies and maybe many, detection would be impossible. This would be because "inter-Magnetic space" that was presented in the description of super-nova and a neutron star could form as a sheath or cocoon around the quasar that no waves of the "Electro magnetic spectrum" could possibly penetrate. Also at greater gravitational contraction if "Gluon field particle inter-inter-space" were to form it would present a more formidable barrier to detection yet.

It follows then that some elliptical galaxies would have the subordinate "Hole" of the quasar completely depleted into the fabric of space and matter and the remaining dominate "Hole" would then be contracting the energy of the galaxy back into the "Hole" as a singularity. The colossal elliptical galaxy M-87 located in the "Virgo cluster" unless a quasar is detected in its core may have a mammoth singularity (Black Hole) fusing stars, the fabric of space and whole galaxies of the "Virgo cluster" back into a singularity of un-believable proportions. The "Big Bang" then is the new fabric of space expanding from the galaxies as "Mini Bangs" and there is no finite age to the Cosmos. The Cosmos is contracting to the density of "Black Holes" as fast as it is expanding to the "Mini-Bangs" of the Galaxies.

In the vast reaches of inter-galactic space there will be in existence "Black Holes of un-imaginable proportions that have contracted all matter as galaxies, and much of the fabric of space into a singularity. In the areas of deep black space where there are no Galaxies, "Gravitons" as the fabric of space" have expanded to the dimension of absolute zero and maybe even beyond. Here Gravitons (Photons, gravaphotons) may have expanded to the true diameter of maybe an inch, a yard, a half mile, maybe a mile, maybe even more. The expansion of particles of the fabric of space around a great "Black Hole" is not because of a "Bang" or a "Big Bang", but rather is due to particles of the fabric of space becoming part of the hole. This again forms a Negative "Gravitational field" of the fabric of space around these great singularities. Each singularity forms a bubble of radically expanded time and dimension as the warped fabric of space to fill the void. The "Gravitational field of a "Black Hole" is a geometrical inversion or negative field of the fabric of space that is the exact opposite of a "Gravitational field" as described by Einstein in the "General theory of Relativity" and was discussed earlier. This gives the "Cosmos a bubbling appearance.

Anything including whole galaxies are pushed away from a large "Black Hole" by the expansion of the particles of the fabric of space around the "Hole". In an extremely large "Black Hole" with a space bubble of maybe a hundred million light years in diameter, galaxies are pushed together into clusters around the great space bubble. Yet they push each other apart by the expanding fabric of new space from each galaxy. The expanding particles of the fabric of space of several extremely large "Super Black Holes" will push clusters of galaxies together into super clusters.

Physical particle dimension as the fabric of space is time and time is physical dimension. Increase particle dimension of the fabric of space and time speeds up. Decrease particle dimension and time slows down. Time speeds up for the fabric of space around a singularity as particle dimension increases. At the surface of the "Hole", particle dimension and time are radically expanded and then they both go through a massive contraction as they are spun into and become part of the "Hole". Particle dimension of the fabric of space contracts and time slows until the fabric of space becomes part of the "Hole" and then time stops with in the "Hole". Directly detecting these great singularities may be next to impossible or almost impossible other than detecting a huge area of space that is void of everything. These great contractions would experience no passage of time and are literally a dead part of the "Cosmos. To enter into a "Black Hole", is to enter into oblivion. When two of them come together they will ignite as a "Super Quasar", that forms a duality of motion that is orientated as rotation to the right, and rotation to the left. Then and only then will the presence and resurrection of a new existence and a new beginning of time and dimension once again be created.

The four forces then do not really exist as fundamental forces in nature. Three of the forces are contractions of the same particle as a Graviton to "Magnetic Particles" and then to "Gluon field Particles". The fourth force is the explosive expansion of dual spin particles as the fission cycle of the strong nuclear force. The strong nuclear force and all releases of energy are the expansion of particles either as singular or dual spin as energy.

The release of energy in any form is one of the true forces of nature. The other true force is fusion or the contraction of

"Gravitational particles" from what we view as the fabric of space to matter. This contraction will continue all the way in to a singularity of motion that is the quantitative substance that is a "Black Hole". In a manor of speaking, the two fundamental forces of nature could be termed as simply "Black" and "White" light.

SECTION—10

THE STRUCTURE OF LIFE ITS SELF

Life, it is all around us. The Neighbors down the street. The crowds of people in a shopping mall. People in Pakistan. Men and women living there lives in Australia. Children playing games in China. A couple out for a short stroll in London England. All over the world people live and play, leading their lives, being born, growing into old age, and finally dying. How life started can not be explained and may never be. If you are a religious person with deep-seated religious beliefs, that may be explanation enough for you. I myself have been an atheist most of my adult life but I have never ever pushed my beliefs onto anybody else or onto other people. I have always felt that it is the right of the individual to believe as they choose. After all, it is the individual that has to live and die with their beliefs whether they are of a religious nature or from the standpoint of an atheist. Development of this theory as "The Theory of Everything" has still not settled the great question as to where did the beginning come from and where is it going. What then is a final conclusion as to the existence of a greater power than we are? No matter what conclusions are derived from a philosophy as an atheist or the religion of religious people, the bottom line says does their have to be a reason for existence and does existence have to have a purpose. Is there a symmetry or pattern to the structure of life? Showing a pattern to the structure of life would not change the philosophy of an atheist or the religious point of view of religious people at all, but may instead provide a much deeper understanding of who and what we are. Like the unification of the four forces of nature as one, may not the religion of religious people and the philosophies of atheism be also unified?

I have a little dog that I think the world of. Animals free in the wild. A pride of lions stalking prey on the plains of Africa.

A great polar bear roaming the frozen arctic wilderness. A troupe of monkeys screaming and screeching high in a tree in the rain forests of Costa Rica. A small kitten kept as a little girl's pet in an apartment in New York City.

This is all life. But this is only part of life. This is only half of the living scheme of things and of life, as we know it. We exist and survive only because of the other half of life. With out the other half of life we would not even be here. The other half of life, is plant life. Our existence is completely dependent on plant life. We consume plant life and the sub species of animal life that consume plant life. We renew our physical structure and replenish the reserves of energy from our ingestion of the other half of life. Plant life! We exhale carbon dioxide and inhale and utilize the oxygen in the atmosphere in our metabolism. Plant life absorbs and utilizes the carbon dioxide that we exhale as a waste product and places oxygen back in the atmosphere that we again utilize in our metabolism.

"DOMINATE SPIN ROTATIONAL ORIENTATION" as a principle of physics simply states that there are two spins or rotations found in nature as orientated to each other and that one spin will dominate over the other. Existence then will be structured to the Dominance of one spin as either matter oriented or as antimatter orientated. The human race is predominately right handed with the electron dominate in the structure of matter over the positron. Our whole existence is structured to this pattern. Animal life is completely dominate over plant life yet animal life can not exist with out plant life and plant life can not exist with out the combustion of animal life. You are a person, a human being with all the emotions, wants, and needs that all people have and still look at how you are structured. You have a right and a left side, a front and a back, and a top as your head and a bottom as your feet. Two axis or rotation as orientated to each other, one turns to the right and one turns to the left as your right and your left sides. You may be right handed, left handed or ambidextrous, but still as a whole the human race is still predominately right handed. You are two axis of rotation as oriented to the earth with your feet on the ground and your head up in the air with a front and a back to your person. There are two halves to your brain with an ego and an alter ego. Your ego as you is dominate over your alter ego although most people listen to there alter ego as there conscience in making decisions in there lives. When we think it is an inter play in between the two egos of our mind in a conscious existence communicating with each other as dual personality. When we communicate with other people, it is through the dominate ego of both persons, relating to each other. Most sub species of life are also structure after the same pattern. Almost all forms of life are a duality with two eyes, two ears, two nose holes, two lungs, legs, fins, tail, a head, and a front and a back.

The sexes are also structured this way. The male is "Dominate" in that the male is usually much heavier built and physically stronger than the female yet before conception the egg in the females womb can become either sex. Sex is determined by sperm from a male that contains sperm of both sexes and is deposited by the male into the female. Which ever sperm, either male or female reaches the egg first and fertilizes it determines the sex of the egg. The unfertilized egg can become either sex as male or female yet there is an equality to the sexes even though the male is much bigger, stronger, and heavier built than the female.

As an example of this, picture a little hundred and ten pound woman with a three hundred-pound football player groveling at her feet. He lavishes her with attention and adoration yet she may spurn and reject him with contempt. If you are a young blade out looking at the pretties and see something that you like, if she does not like you, you may as well take your genes and go some place else. You do not have a prayer with her no matter how big and strong you are. This is true not only in our own species, but most of the subspecies as well. One spin will dominate over the other, yet there is an equality of separate spin orientations in all facets of life to each other that intertwine back and forth that weave a pattern that we call a consciences of equality and a sense of egotistical well being. Nothing is ever equal and yet everything is equal. Always there is dominance of one spin over the other and yet the dominance of one facet of life will equal the dominance of another. What is subordinate in one place, will be equalized by dominance in another. The three hundred-pound football player could grab the little one hundred and ten-pound woman with one hand and physically crush and over power her with ease. Yet he does not and in the twilight years of life she may out live him by a substantial amount. He will salve his bruised ego for a while and then maybe find that certain little someone that thinks he's great and they could live happily ever after.

"DOMINATE SPIN ROTATIONAL ORIENTATION". God and the Devil. Right and wrong. Good and evil. One spin will dominate. Adolph Hitler and the rise and fall of the Nazi regime. This is atheism in its darkest possible form. This is atheism in one of the most vile and brutal interpretations possible. With a few strokes of a pen, Adolph Hitler condemned six million people to a senseless degenerate existence that deprived them of all human rights and then the blackness of death in one of the most gruesome mass murders ever perpetuated on the human race.

First the people were striped naked, men women and children, and then led like sheep to the gas chambers where their minds and bodies were destroyed. The corpses were then thrown into the nightmarish blast furnaces of Hitler's hellish regime, which reduced them to pitiful amounts of unrecognizable ash with all the dignities of their personalities and identities lost forever. You talk about the mass killing power of atomic weapons; this monster of a man murdered six million people and tortured countless others to death with just a very small motion of his hand. Right can become left and left can become right. But one spin will dominate. Good can become evil and evil can become good. Atheism as defined by most atheists is an effort to seek out the truth of reality. To gain an intellectual understanding of what constitutes the truth and then use this truth to grasp a true meaning of the basic simplicities of right and wrong. What Adolph Hitler did was nothing more than a brutal senseless act as a degenerate form of egotism coupled with a fanatic abuse of absolute power.

Not only can atheism become a twisted form of ideology, but religion it's self can also go full circle and loose all site of what it was meant to stand for in the first place. Most religions are meant to stand for the better things in life. To give guidance, comfort, an explanation, and a meaning to existence that people can follow in leading their lives but not all religions have done this. As an example, a high priest of the Incas or Aztecs religion that offers human sacrifice to the sun god takes three small children to a mountaintop on a beautiful warm sunny day. This yellow coward of a man then rips open the abdomen of one of the hapless screaming children with a stone knife and tears out the child's living heart. He then holds the child's beating heart with the blood of innocence streaming down his arms up to the sky in the warm tropical sunshine. The other two children screaming in terror are both slaughtered as offerings to the raging thermonuclear furnace riding high in the sky that is ninety three million miles away from it all. What a brutal cowardly futile senseless act of murder all in the name of religion. Better that this coward of a man were to rip open his own breast with the stone knife and tear out his own beating heart sacrificing himself to his pagan god than to hide behind the slaughter of innocent children as sacrifices to nothing.

The pope as the leader of the "Catholic Church" instigated the inquisition. The inquisition all in the name of God almighty burned thousands of people at the stake for heresy and tortured countless others to death. It has been said that the Spanish inquisition perfected the art of torture. It has been said that a skilled torturer was capable of extracting every last visage of pain from their victims before death stilled their torment. Religion in instigating the inquisition became as evil as Adolph Hitler did in his senseless murder of six million people. Again, spin to the right can become spin to the left, and spin to the left can become spin to the right. But one spin will dominate. You have to keep the correct perspective from an intellectual standpoint as to what constitutes the true difference between what is really right, and what is really wrong.

"DOMINATE SPIN ROTATIONAL ORIENTATION". Our whole existence is shaped by this pattern. We make decisions. If we are unable to come to a decision then we have a crisis. Whatever the crisis is, it will have to be resolved before our activity can continue. One spin will dominate over the other or it becomes a stalemate. All our games and activities are structured this way. Take a prizefight! What kind of a prizefight would it be if there was only one fighter in the ring? Nothing will happen with only one fighter in the ring. One fighter is a singularity. There has to be two or a duality of motion in order for there to be a contest. Very seldom is there a draw. If there is a draw, then they will most likely have to fight again at a later date in order to determine a winner. In most bouts, one fighter will win and one will lose. The structure of a football game, only this time there are two groups of players in teams. The pattern is still the same. At the end of the game, one team will win and one will lose. This great symmetrical pattern follows through into politics and political fights, in a court of law with the prosecution and the defense, and even countries or nations waging war with each other. Anything you can think of in our existence will follow the same pattern.

The symmetry and dominance of either right or left is the single greatest truth in existence and yet because it is so ingrained into our existence, we do not see it for what it is. It has been shown how it starts with the formation of electrons and positrons and then neutrinos and anti-neutrinos. One spin will dominate as either right or left and existence will be created as either matter of anti-matter. There are six possible spin combinations as orientated that are the six Quarks of the standard model of nuclear physics and eight combinations of gluon spin that are the eight gluons.

The contraction again goes from photon (Gravaphoton) (G), as the fabric of what we call space, to magnetic particle (M) and what we call matter. It continues then to Gluon field particle (E) that holds matter (M) together. The final contraction is to a singularity of motion as the gravitational quantitative substance that forms as a “Black Star” or “Black Hole”. (B) When two “Black Holes” or “Black stars” as singularities come together they ignite as a Quasar and the duality of existence is again created and has come full circle.

Anything can be read as an interpretation into what has been written in this book. The title of this book, is “THE THEORY OF EVERYTHING”. If you are a religious person, it can be interpreted as proof of the resurrection and the existence of God. If you are an atheist, claims can be made to support a point of view as a non-believer of religion, but be careful that both do not go full circle. Religion could become a form of atheism and atheism become a form of religion. Again, right can become left and left can become right. The great question that still remains is, was there ever a true beginning, and will there ever be a true and final end? Or does time start, stop and go backward in a great fantastic arc that we will never understand. Is there a great and all-powerful intellectual entity in existence that created a Graviton?

SECTION—11

Two fish in the ocean look at each other, and the water between them appears as space to the fish. We know that the space is filled with water, and that the fish are made of about 97% water and about 03% something else. The fish don't know this though, and are not aware that they are in a medium, and are composed mostly of the medium that they are in.

As the intellectual species, of the living evolutionary process of our existence, we are aware of the fish, the atmosphere, and much of the physical structure of our world. With all of this awareness, mankind has been no more aware of the "Gravitational Aether" as a physical medium than we were at one time that the earth that we live on, is round, and not flat. There was a period in the history of mankind's orientation to our position within the scope of reality, when it was universally believed that the earth was flat.

Physicists in trying to understand the mysteries of gravity have proclaimed that you can never see gravity, that you can never see a graviton. The truth is, you see gravity all of the time and every day of your life. The very act of seeing as has been presented is by the propagation of the "Electro magnetic spectrum" as expanding contracting photons as particles of light and gravity. The very structural wave nature of light its self is an alternating fission fusion reaction of the nuclear forces. Fission is the expanding nuclear force that we see as light, and fusion is the contracting nuclear force that we see as blackness. An expanding contracting Photon as a Graviton as a particle of the "Gravitational Aether" is what we are part of and exist in. It is the fundamental substance that we are made of.

Go into a dark room and see the shadows on the wall and the rays of light coming in through the window. All that you see as light are gravity waves of the "Gravitational Aether". All that you see as darkness are either neutral or contracting gravitons. When we see white light or the beautiful colors of the rainbow, or the gray and blackness of a dark night, we are actually seeing Gravity. If you have ever been deep into a cave, you know how dark and black it can be in there. The blackness you see, are particles of the "Gravitational Aether" in its neutral or contracting state.

Go back into the light and place your hand in front of your face. It looks as though there is nothing between your hand and your face. Now move your hand back and forth. You still do not feel anything and it looks as though there is absolutely nothing between your hand and your face. Touch your face with your hand and you will swear that there is nothing between your hand and your face but space and the atmosphere.

Put your hand down and snap it hard. Now do it over again only this time harder. Now you can feel the presence of the "Gravitational Aether". If you snap it to hard, it is going to hurt. The "Gravitational Aether" is there all around us and stretches from us to all of eternity. We are solidly locked and geared to its cosmic presence by the explosive expansive pressure of the "Big Bang" or a "Bang". What we perceive as space when matter reaches the speed of light is as solid in its own context as what we perceive as matter. We can move freely through it at sub-light velocities as long as we do not attempt to bully it around. If we try to move to rapidly or to stop to quickly, the awesome incredible power of the "Gravitational Aether" as the "Cosmic Sea" we are part of and live in will make its presence known.

The thermonuclear reaction, in the detonation of a Hydrogen bomb, is the expansive, explosive "Big Bang" power of the "Gravitational Aether" and is the same medium that hurt your hand when you snapped it too hard. You actually felt a very small part of the tremendous explosive power of the "Gravitational Aether" when you made too rapid a motion with your hand. Mankind on a cosmic scale of intellect, has been no more aware of the true reality of our being, than the two fish in the sea, that did not know that they are in water as a medium, and are composed mostly of the water that they are in.

ABOUT THE AUTHOR

When I was about ten years old, they had a class on astronomy in grade school and I was crazy about it. I loved it and it has stuck with me all my life. Science, physics, and especially Astronomy have always been of great interest to me. I am now an old man, 71 years of age, but when the opportunity during the course of my life has arisen, I have always diligently pursued my great interests. I now own my home in the Arizona desert far from the light pollution of any major city. I have a 12 inch Schmidt Cassegrain telescope and a small private observatory for the telescope in my back yard right behind my house. I have two CCD imaging cameras that are coupled to two computers and am engaged in Astro-imaging of deep sky objects.

Gravity has always held a unique fascination for me. What could this mysterious invisible force be that held everything together so gently and yet with such great force. 1990 was a year that after an early retirement I had some time to again pursue my great interests. As I though out the aspects of how gravity could function, I became convinced that gravity had to be composed of particles (A graviton) and that the only way this could work is for gravity to push and for the fabric of space to actually physically move.

I was discouraged on every front. The "Theories of Relativity" were so complicated and "Quantum theories" were just about as bad. I bought books on all aspects of science, made trips to the public library for more books, and subscribed to scientific and astronomical magazines and I read and studied them all. I wrote to several professors at major universities who were good enough to answer me and was told that if I could not put my ideas into a mathematical form that no body would listen to me or take me serious. This I have found out to be true so I decided to write this book. From about 1990 to the present time, which is about ten years, I wrote, studied, and rewrote over and over again the text of this book.

It was not meant to be in the beginning but the ideas that I pursued became what I honestly believe to be the structure of "The Theory of Everything" that Physicists worldwide are looking for. Whether I have or not is for you the reader to understand and then decide. There are no equations or mathematics in this book. The text is strictly a description of the structure of the "Cosmos" starting with a Graviton as a particle of gravity and progressing upwards to the galaxies. The description given in this book is for what I believe an idea that turned out to be a TOE. A TOE is a 'THEORY OF EVERYTHING.' A "THEORY OF EVERYTHING" is a realistic approach and a symmetrical description of everything that is in existence including the very structure of life it's self.

www.ingramcontent.com/pod-product-compliance
Ingram Content Group UK Ltd.
Pitfield, Milton Keynes, MK11 3LW, UK
UKHW040016200726
13854UKWH00001B/233

9 780759 675650